If You Don't Ask The Answer Is No:

A Practical Guide for Getting Through College
Without Falling Through the Cracks

Noelle,

Keep shining your
light.

— Rich Schlesinger

Copyright © 2021 by Rich A. Schlesinger, Ed.D.

Published and Distributed in USA and CANADA by LLH Publishing Inc. www.andreaseydel.com

Library of Congress Cataloging-in-Publication Data

Schlesinger, Rich A.

If You Don't Ask The Answer Is No: A Practical Guide for Getting Through College Without Falling Through the Cracks

1.Nonfiction-Education & Teaching-Administration -2. Non-Fiction-Education-College Guides.

ISBN- 978-1-9991409-5-3

1st Printing: May 2021. Printed in USA.

Proofreader: Lindy Bailey

Publisher's Note & Author DISCLAIMER

If You Don't Ask The Answer Is No:

A Practical Guide for Getting Through College
Without Falling Through the Cracks

Rich A. Schlesinger, Ed.D.

Dedication

In loving memory of my mother, Deborah Lee Schlesinger, a champion for civil rights and an advocate for social justice.

If You Don't Ask The Answer Is No:

A Practical Guide for Getting Through College
Without Falling Through the Cracks

CONTENTS

Part 3: CREATING AN ADVOCACY ACTION PLAN FOR CAMPUS LIFE

Part 4: BONUS FOR PARENTS! ENRICHING THE CAMPUS EXPERIENCE FROM A PARENT'S PERSPECTIVE

What is Parental Advocacy?
Understand You Through and Through
   Helicopter Parenting
   Snowplow Parenting
   The Uninvolved or Neglectful Parent
   Balance Reaching Out with Keeping Out
   Mental Health Challenges Facing Today's Parents and Their Children
   What Parenting Style Works Best and Why
   From Tough Love to Enough Love: How to Successfully Parent Your College Student
What Not to Do
The Parental Advocacy Tool Kit

INTRODUCTION

As a lifelong educator with over 25 years' experience in higher education settings, including as a placement officer, career counselor, academic advisor, a college administrator managing the Career Services office at a community college, and an adjunct faculty member in the Humanities, student advocacy has always been near and dear to my heart. I have seen many students come and go over the years, some of whom have made a lasting impression on me, and I still cherish the privilege of teaching them and empowering them to be their best selves.

I have answered many questions, graded papers – too many to mention – conducted individual conferences, and advised countless students about their career and life goals. To be expected, it goes with the territory. One thing forever etched in my mind is all the questions that did not get asked! We have been students in a class in which the teacher asks – often in a perfunctory manner and with little time for pause – does anybody have any questions? And all too often, a deafening silence falls over the room. I have been that professor many times in my career. In the beginning, I made the mistake of assuming that, well, I guess that means my lecture was absolutely crystal clear since no one asked a question. I could not have been more wrong! Of course, there were questions!! It is just that many students, for whatever reason, are not equipped to ask them. Maybe they are timid, they do not know what they do not know, or perhaps I did not pause long enough to allow them time for reflection; or they quite simply never learned the value of advocating for themselves. I have witnessed many students confide in me about complaints concerning other professors, peers, administrators, etc. Often, most of these students assumed that they had to "live with it" if they had a problem. Sometimes I would explain to them the process and the protocol for documenting and reporting an issue. Other times, I would direct them to the Student Code of Conduct for further reference. I have often wondered if any students ever actually read the Student Code of Conduct. It would be akin to reading the Apple iPhone disclaimers when you register your phone. An exercise in futility, should you choose to undertake it. And let's be honest, most students do not. Student Codes of Conduct contain voluminous amounts of information and legalese that even the most erudite student would have a hard time deciphering.

I have thought a lot about advocacy over the years. How it is all too often swept under the rug and trivialized by those in positions of power. Students are frequently ill-equipped to navigate the complex bureaucracy that exists in many colleges and universities today. Perhaps, they decide that it is best to appease those in power and tell their professors what they think they want to hear for fear of repercussions and reprisals. Just do what you need to do to get that all-important degree and so you can move on to greener pastures. And that does not bode well for future generations. Do we want to be churning out students for whom self-advocacy is merely an afterthought? Are we cultivating a culture of lackeys and sycophants? If we are, I certainly do not want to be a part of it. And so that became the impetus for this book. My goal in writing this book is to lay the groundwork for a simple, user-friendly guide to advocacy for students and parents alike. In addition, I have added a special bonus (Part 4) for parents of college students. I hope you find the information helpful.

-Rich Schlesinger, November 2020

PART 1

HARNESS THE POWER OF SELF-ADVOCACY ON CAMPUS

"If you haven't the strength to impose your own terms upon life, then you must accept the terms it offers you."
-T.S. Elliot

What is Self-Advocacy?

If you are a college student or a parent reading this book, you probably wonder: what is self-advocacy and why should it matter to me? The first thing you should know is that self-advocacy is a complex, complicated, and challenging process. Not only is it hard to articulate – especially for a college student – but it is also difficult to measure. But that does not mean it does not exist. As Einstein once said: "Just because something cannot be measured does not mean that it does not exist." Self-advocacy is one of the most critical components of a student's success, and its impact extends far beyond your college experience. Self-advocacy fosters greater independence, self-efficacy, autonomy, and empowerment (Grutta 2018). It allows students to discover, define, and articulate their identities as learners and ask for and receive the help they need and are entitled to as part of their college experience.

Self-advocacy also serves as a motivator. When a student sees firsthand the benefits of their advocacy, they are motivated to continue advocating on their behalf, which creates a positive pattern and a feeling of empowerment, freedom, and independence. In short, it is a gateway to liberation and adulthood during one of the most exciting periods in your life: college!

Self-advocacy is not easy. It is hard! Think about it. How many times have you sat in a high school or college classroom, and you felt like what the teacher has just told you is not clear, but you said nothing? You were afraid to ask. Maybe you thought your question would come across as dumb to the other students. So, you just decided to keep quiet. You get another chance at the end of the class when the professor asks the requisite "any questions." But you still cannot summon the nerve to speak up. So, you let your question or concern come to pass. And low and behold, it becomes an issue on the test. The test question(s) is not straightforward because you did not clarify something in class.

Consequently, your grade is adversely affected because you failed to speak up and advocate for yourself. That is just one of many examples of how advocacy – or lack thereof – can have a profound impact on your college experience. Anxiety can be a roadblock and a barrier that often impedes students' ability to advocate for themselves. Although college can be one of the most exciting times of one's young life, it can also be a time of soul searching and identity seeking when students grapple with self-acceptance, shame, embarrassment, and fear of failure. Advocacy, therefore, is a process that one cannot master overnight. It takes time.

Students are often reluctant to advocate for themselves because they feel they would be inconveniencing their professors. Perhaps it is a part of our psyche and its human nature to not want to rock the boat. But if we think of advocacy as ensuring that we are getting the most out of our college experience – the things we are entitled to as paying customers of the college or university – it is not rocking the boat after all. It is merely asserting our rights and ensuring that they are protected. Nothing wrong with that.

I have experienced firsthand this reluctance by students to advocate for themselves many times. Often, it manifests itself in a simple email exchange. I cannot count the number of emails I have received over the years, beginning with something like this: "Sorry to bother you". My first thought – and invariably my first response – is you are not "bothering" me at all. I am here as a resource for you! I recall hearing the same refrain from students who have dropped by my office during office hours. Some students are just wired to feel as if asking for help is an imposition on your time. And it should not ever feel that way. Ultimately, we (college staff, faculty, and administrators) are here to serve you!! And any college staff member who does not believe that is his or her primary mission should be shown the door. If you work in a college and do not believe in putting students first, it is time for a career change!

Many advising departments identify self-advocacy as one of their top ten learning outcomes for first-year students. For students to evolve to a level in which they feel comfortable advocating for themselves, they must become self-aware of their learning strengths and challenges. And many first-year freshman seminar courses include an advocacy component in which students are encouraged to set personal and academic goals and then demonstrate their capacity to advocate for themselves.

In my first-year freshman seminar course, I include an advocacy component. I ask students to contact their advisors and conduct an interview with them. They typically ask questions related to student success: How do you define student success? What steps should I be taking to ensure a successful semester? They also ask about the advisor's educational background and how they got to be where they are today. They are then required to present their findings to the class. I hope that this exercise fosters a deeper connection between the student and his or her advisor and empowers them to see the value in advocating for themselves. Also, I ask students to identify a position they wish to interview for, and then I have the class conduct a mock interview with each student. Among the questions, a couple causally relate to advocacy: Why should I hire you? What separates you from other students with similar qualifications? If you have been fortunate enough to develop the capacity for advocacy throughout your college career, you will be much better prepared to answer both questions. I will add more on this subject in the next section.

When school violence has occurred on college campuses – most notably the Brock Turner sexual assault case at Stanford University in 2015 and Brandon Vandenburg of Vanderbilt University in 2016 – an increasing number of students have come forward to speak out against school violence. Thus, there has been increased attention and focus directed toward helping students seek support if an incident occurs and to exercise their right to speak out and advocate against the injustices committed. With a plethora of information only a few clicks away, today's students can access lots of information almost instantaneously. Consequently, they awaken to existing inequalities much faster than previous generations. Indeed, the student response to these cases was swift and reverberated across campus and the country. Students in both cases advocated for changes in attitudes and policies. Ultimately, they inspired the public to take notice which eventually led to the colleges and universities instituting significant changes to their policies.

As these cases have demonstrated, one benefit of acquiring self-advocacy skills is that they can be a conduit for supporting changes that students wish to see in their institutions and beyond. It may well be the most crucial foundation skill that leads to success in college. Students who thrive in college tend to do so when they feel a "connection" with the institution. Virtually every study worth its weight on student retention has supported this claim. And one of the best ways to feel a connection with your college is to identify a cause you believe in and advocate for it!

For students who may require additional support, such as added time for tests, curriculum modifications, one-on-one learning, etc., advocacy is of paramount importance. It may involve ensuring that one has the educational resources he or she needs, ensuring that the professor understands his or her diagnosis, and is making all reasonable accommodations as outlined in the student's Individual Educational Plan (IEP). But it is much more than just ensuring that reasonable accommodations are in place. Self-advocacy is also about knowing when and how to take effective action if difficulties arise. It means working within the system, knowing when and how to challenge the system if need be, while at the same time demonstrating independence. Sometimes students with learning disabilities can feel alienated by colleges and universities. And it is not always intentional. Remember, full-time professors often have five or more classes with 20 or more students in each of them.

In some cases, this number can be closer to 300 than 20. So, it is not inconceivable that the professor may not be fully aware of the nature of your learning disability. Therefore, it is incumbent upon you, the student, to take the initiative and advocate for yourself. Never assume someone will do it for you.

A few years ago, I had a student in my speech class who had a significant stutter when she spoke. To make matters worse, she was an international student for whom English was not her first language. Her English was ok, but she was not yet completely comfortable with the language, and at times, struggled with the translation of idiomatic expressions, among other things. After the first class, this student confided in me that she had emigrated to the U.S. on a student visa to escape persecution in her home country. She had received death threats from extremists for some of her social media posts advocating for women's rights. Although she did not provide documentation for her stutter, which she attributed to anxiety resulting from the trauma of psychological abuse from her father, I was very aware of it. I always made sure she had extra time to speak – and did not penalize her for it – and I took that into account when evaluating her speeches. As it turned out, she demonstrated an ability to stay within the required time limit after the first speech and still convey the thoughts she wished to express. It was clear to me that she was a very bright student who had aspired to become a physician. I had – and still have – no doubt that she will achieve her goal. However, she was often at odds with other students in the class. She was adamantly opposed to all organized religion, and it just so happened this class was composed of several religious conservatives and Evangelical Christians. As you might expect, this led to many intense discussions about the merits of religion and creationism. As a professor, I often had to intervene to keep the class on track. Moreover, she decided to use her speeches as an opportunity to unleash her vitriol against all religions. Consequently, her speeches ended up almost 20 minutes over the required time limit! And she decided to use speeches two through five to advance her anti-religious agenda.

I explained to her, verbally and in writing as stated in the syllabus, that there would be time penalties for exceeding the time limit after each speech. I also made it clear that I would consider her stutter and make it a point to be lenient with grading. Ultimately, I gave her a break with her grade by limiting the number of points deducted for exceeding the time limit. Nevertheless, this ended up lowering her two-letter grades. At the end of the semester, I submitted my final grades and thought that was the end of it. Fast forward six months, and I received an email from her asking why I lowered her grade.

I asked her why she waited six months before inquiring — or advocating — about her grade if this was so important to her. She immediately fired back what seemed like an angry email explaining that she did not think I would be available after the class was over until the next semester, and that is why she waited six months to contact me. She also reiterated that she had a stutter and felt like I had not taken that into account when calculating her grade. I explained to her that not only did I take it into account, but I gave her a big break concerning grading. I could have taken off 40 or more points on each of her speeches. Still, I decided to cap my deduction at 20 points per speech on account of her stutter — even though she did not provide documentation. I extended her an invitation to discuss the matter further and reach out to the dean of our department (my boss) if she felt it was necessary. Her response was another angry email stating that I was not fair and that she would speak with the dean and the president. Was this an example of effective self-advocacy? I am not so sure. Threatening people is never a good idea. But at the end of the day, I genuinely appreciated the fact that she had the presence of mind to advocate for herself, even if that made things a bit uncomfortable and stressful for me as an instructor. I have no ill will towards this student and wish her nothing but the best. So, the moral is, when in doubt, speak out! Even if it makes things uncomfortable for all parties involved.

Self-advocacy aims to help students transition into successful adulthood and equip them with the skills necessary to navigate their chosen career. Long before self-advocacy became an integral part of freshman orientation programs, Charles Drake, founder of Landmark College in Putney, VT, framed the concept in 1985 using the simple verbiage: "Don't do for the student what the student can do for him/herself." (D'Alessio and Osterholt 2018) The philosophy behind that statement is the belief that each student will become a self-advocate provided they have the proper tools to succeed (D'Alessio and Osterholt 2018). Learning how to self-advocate permeates every aspect of student life. It begins with explicit instruction in a student's first year and continues through the duration of their college time.

It can be a challenge for many students who lack experience combined with the effects of well-meaning parents who advocate for their students rather than allowing them to take on this responsibility themselves. I will have more to say about this issue in Part 3.

Ideally, I believe that instructors should introduce self-advocacy skills within an advising program's curriculum during a student's first semester. Advisors should work with the student to facilitate knowledge acquisition, define self-advocacy, differentiate between entitlement and self-advocacy, assess the student's knowledge of basic college practices (these include grading systems, intranet tools, college policies such as course add/drop, and withdrawal periods), and a discussion should take place about how to communicate with faculty regarding coursework concerns. Students should be made aware of the benefits of effective self-advocacy with parents, and they should understand the benefits of accessing college resources.

What Would College Look Like if I Did Not Advocate for Myself?

For the sake of argument, let us suppose this book never made it to your inbox or your doorstep, and for whatever reason, you never quite fully embraced the power of advocacy. How would your college experience be different? Enter the internet armchair warrior, aka, IACW. We all know the type. The person who rants incessantly on his or her favorite social media platform about the world's ills or the latest grievance du jour but never actually does anything about it. If you do not learn to advocate for yourself, your future may align with the internet armchair warrior! There may come a time when you reflect on your college experience, and all you can do is sit around and talk about what could've and would've, and it may well be your greatest regret!

If you do not learn to self-advocate, your college experience may be much less fulfilling. Imagine a typical day would look something like this: go to class, return to your dorm or apartment, play a few videos games, stare at your phone for a few hours, maybe get a workout in if you are fitness minded, fire off a few texts, do your homework (hopefully), and rinse and repeat. Yet, something will feel like it is missing. You may feel like you are merely going through the motions to an end; the end is getting your degree so that you can be more marketable to employers and ultimately lock up that dream job you have been hoping for since you decided to enroll in college. You may feel somewhat alienated from your peers and feel like you do not have an authentic connection with your college. And thus, you may be at greater risk of withdrawing. Remember, the number one reason students withdraw from college has less to do with finance and more to do with a lack of a connection. So, do not become an Internet Armchair Warrior. As the embattled filmmaker Woody Allen once said, "90% of success is just showing up." So, make it a point to show up somewhere – anywhere really – and advocate for yourself. For example, you might decide to attend one of the many study skills workshops offered on campus or virtually, just to familiarize yourself with some of the resources available to you through student services. Remember, not only are you entitled to these services, but you are also paying for them, albeit indirectly, through your student activities fees that are a part of your college tuition. So, you might as well get what you pay for, right?

Perhaps you decide to venture over to the Student Activities Office or browse their web page to see what student clubs are available. Ok, so you may be thinking right about now; I do not have the time for all this extracurricular stuff. I have a full-time job, and I am carrying 15 credits this semester; and there are only so many hours in a day, so self-advocacy is not happening for me. Fair enough, you may well have some tough decisions to make. And obviously, you need to support yourself — especially if you are the sole financier of your college education. But be advised, often, you have more time than you think you do, even if it is only one extra hour per week. For the record, I did my best work in college when I was the busiest — when I had 2 or 3 jobs, I was enrolled in 16 credits, and played a sport (hockey). It seems a bit counterintuitive: if your plate is full of extracurricular activity, then you probably have less time to study, and thus, your grades may suffer. But the opposite was true — at least for me. Because I had structure and I felt more "connected" to the college, I felt more empowered — and motivated — to immerse myself in my studies. And I ultimately did my best work when I was the busiest, and I should add, my worst work when I had too much time on my hands!

So, it behooves you to immerse yourself in your studies and extracurricular activities, and advocate for yourself.

Why Should Advocacy Matter to Me and How Can It Make Me More Marketable to Employers?

We are all motivated by different things. For some people, it is about making a difference or becoming enlightened. Others may aspire to make a lot of money or are motivated by the desire for recognition and approval. All these things have value. Whatever your primary motivations are, you will need to give some thought to how you will make yourself more marketable to employers. You will, after all, need to start planning for a career at some point. Unless, of course, you plan on spending your post-college years on your parent's couch, popcorn in hand, with Netflix movies at the ready.

Enter self-advocacy. Self-advocacy will not only teach you how to take the initiative on your own, assert your rights, and stick up for yourself, but it will indeed make you more marketable to employers, and thus, more likely that you will get hired by one. I always tell aspiring job seekers to imagine if they are the one asking the questions, i.e., the prospective employer(s) or search committee who must decide whether they want to hire you. As part of the interviewing process, they may be interviewing dozens or more candidates. And to preserve the integrity and fairness of the process, they are required to ask each candidate the same questions. One of the more common interview questions, which would apply to virtually any position, is this: "Tell me what separates you from other candidates with similar education and experience?" Invariably, employers and search committees ask this question to get a response that goes something like this: "I am hardworking, reliable, dependable ... and blah, blah, blah." Still awake? You get the idea. Although this answer may be right and perhaps even an accurate representation of who you are, it does not necessarily distinguish you from countless other candidates. Of course, you are hardworking, reliable, and dependable! Would anybody choose to state the opposite? I am lazy, unreliable, and you probably can't count on me when you need me!

Suppose you have dedicated your college career to self-advocacy. In that case, it will be not only a great conversation starter with any prospective employer, but more importantly, it will separate you from the "hardworking, reliable, and dependable" crowd. Remember, from the employer's perspective it is much easier to find something wrong with you than to find something right with you. If he or she interviews two dozen candidates, and all say I am hardworking, reliable, and dependable, and they all have excellent grades and stellar letters of recommendation, how do they decide who to hire? They do need to choose eventually. So naturally, they will begin to fish for flaws – trust me, as someone who served on many a hiring committee, it can indeed feel like a fishing expedition – to differentiate one "hardworking, reliable, and dependable" candidate from another.

When you answer the question, "What separates you from other candidates with similar education and experience?" your answer may sound something like this: "Well, for starters, I was never one to sit back and absorb all the information. Nor did I simply just accept everything my professors told me as the ultimate truth. I took the time to develop my critical thinking skills. I took the initiative and advocated for myself from the very first day I set foot on campus right up until graduation." At this point, you should be prepared to elaborate with some degree of specificity. Perhaps that means you made it a point to visit your professor regularly during office hours to assess your progress and determine what additional work, if any, you could be doing to help your grade. Maybe you inquired about the reliability and validity of specific test questions, or questioned the methodology used in creating the exam. Perhaps you conducted an exhaustive search of all financial aid resources available to you. Your search may have included grants and scholarships available in the private sector that you didn't know about initially. Maybe you decided to enroll in a study skills course, even though you were already a good student, to avail yourself of all the resources available to you. Maybe you advocated for better housing conditions in your dorm room. And remember, your adventures in advocacy need not be antagonistic. Your goal is not to rock the boat – it is merely to advocate for all services you are entitled to have. If you do that civilly and in good faith, you will not feel guilty. Equally important, you may have decided to set foot in the Career Services office at your college. Career Services is the office that helps students figure out what they want to do and then helps them get there. Bear in mind, all these services are free, but you do pay for them indirectly as part of your student activities fees attached to your tuition. So, you might as well advocate for yourself and utilize them. Otherwise, you will not be getting the most bang for your buck.

A Case Study in Advocacy

I do not claim to be an expert in financial aid, scholarships, loans, grants, or graduate assistantships. However, I was fortunate enough to have applied for and been awarded an all-expense-paid graduate assistantship which enabled me to complete my master's degree debt-free. I will have a bit more to say about financial aid in Part 2 of this book, but I do want to shed some light on the case of Henry Bazakas as an example of when self-advocacy can be so critically important.

Henry Bazakas was a third-generation college student from Berkeley, California, who enrolled at the University of California Berkeley as a walk-on offensive lineman on the Cal football team (Witz 2020, B8). An accomplished athlete in his own right, Henry also happened to be an erudite scholar. He received an award for having the team's highest grade point average on three separate occasions. In collaboration with another teammate, Henry coordinated a summer reading program at a local elementary school. He even won an award for his commitment to strength and conditioning while recovering from a torn knee ligament. Henry Bazakas is an extremely talented, emerging young professional with a bright future ahead of him.

But like so many of us today, Henry had health concerns — and rightfully so — related to the Coronavirus pandemic. So, he contacted his coach, Justin Wilcox, to inform him that he was opting out of his final season due to these health concerns. What followed highlighted the often-conflicting agendas and interests of the business side of college football — and the push to play at all costs, even during a pandemic — pitted against the educational and academic needs of students served by the program.

After informing his coach he was opting out of his final season, Bazakas learned that his scholarship had been cut. He was then billed for more than $24,000.00 halfway through his summer term because the athletic department had revoked the financial aid it had already paid! Can you imagine the look on his face upon receiving a bill for $24,000.00? He was led to believe that his scholarship would cover this expense.

To his credit, Bazakas appealed. A university appeals committee ruled that the school had violated N.C.A.A. rules by abruptly pulling his aid before giving him an opportunity for a hearing. He also asked for his scholarship back for the fall semester, but the appeals panel sided with the athletic department's decision not to renew it. At the time, Bazakas said that: "It feels like the second I was done playing football, the program was done with me" (Witz 2020, B8).

It turns out that the university decided to restore Bazaka's summer aid after it ruled that the financial aid office canceled it due to a "clerical" error. Surprisingly, this so-called "clerical error" did not come to light until the New York Times conducted an inquiry in mid-October, a month after the committee's initial ruling. Sometimes all the self-advocacy in the world will not amount to a hill of beans. You must get the media involved. Case in point. Bazakas has since stated that no one from Cal had bothered to contact him to acknowledge what the university has characterized as an honest mistake.

To be clear, Henry Bazakas had opted out of his final college football season at a time of great uncertainty for college football players and other college athletes. Some schools require athletes to sign liability waivers upon returning to campus for summer workouts (Witz 2020, B8). It was weeks before conferences like the Big Ten, the Pac-12, and the Southeastern Conferences said they would honor scholarships for athletes who opted out. The N.C.A.A. did not make it a blanket policy until August. Standard scholarship agreements state that athletes can have their aid canceled if they withdraw from a team.

According to Bazakas, "You are supposed to make every decision for the team and that is what you want, but at some point, you're an individual. You're not really allowed to advocate for yourself." Perhaps most tellingly, "You don't realize you can until you're out of the system" (Witz 2020, B8). Fortunately, some good results came from Bazakas's case. Two close friends on the team, offensive lineman Valentino Daltoso and Jake Curhan, emerged as leaders of a movement composed of Pac-12 players. They advocated for more rights for players, including having a say on health protocols and protections for athletes who chose to sit out a season. Also, Andrew Cooper, who ran cross country at Washington State and Cal, and had been an organizer in the students' rights movement, said that Bazakas's case was one of the many discussed among hundreds of players across the country in group conversations through video conferencing. A great example of self-advocacy in action!

Cooper has stated that "Ninety-nine percent of college athletes stay silent about the injustices they experience. We're told, 'Just be grateful.' When it comes down to it, no one is there to protect us, because athletic departments' financial interests do not align with athletes' interests. It underscores why self-advocacy is so important. Many athletic departments are banking on the fact that most students will not advocate for themselves and that they will remain silent and 'just be grateful.'"

When Bazakas had called his coach, he was unaware of an important date: July 1, when the N.C.A.A. requires schools to notify athletes of any roster reductions for the next academic year (Witz 2020, B8). The financial aid office did not refer to the date in the financial aid agreement that Bazakas signed for 2019-2020. An athletic department spokesman acknowledged that Bazakas had not been aware of Cal's deadline, but he claimed that the coach had told the player not to expect a renewal.

About summer aid: each school makes its own decisions. This summer Cal was much more fiscally conservative. The athletic department faced a 55 million dollar deficit if no fall sports were permitted, so they mostly restricted athletes to one summer class because of coronavirus-related budget constraints (Witz 2020, B8).

But Bazakas's case appeared to be an exception. He had received a text on May 18 from

Joel Derechnisky, the team's academic coordinator, who asked if he needed to take all three classes he had registered for during the summer semester. Bazakas indicated that he wanted to have his final two courses for the fall semester during the season. Derechinsky said that would be ok. A month later, Bazakas received notice that he would no longer be on scholarship. Upon checking his account, he discovered two new charges: $23,506 for summer fees and $631 for the summer stipend (Witz 2020, B8).

With the help of family friends, including a lawyer, he filed his appeal. The athletic department initially countered his plea by offering part of his summer aid back. A three-person committee overseeing the appeals process sided with Bazakas. Indeed, the athletic department failed to provide a hearing, and due process before the college initially revoked his aid. N.C.A.A. rules required this.

Bob Jacobsen, an undergraduate dean on the committee, said that Bazakas's aid was restored because Cal's policy does not support aid revoked during a term. And the athletic department discovered that Bazakas's courses were incorrectly classified as beginning in late July rather than in May, which apparently, caused the initial revocation of his aid. I would be willing to bet that 99.99% of students would not have known anything about this unless they took the time to advocate for themselves.

PART 2

EVERYTHING THAT YOU NEVER KNEW YOU ARE ENTITLED TO ON CAMPUS

"Colleges and universities should be safe havens where ruthless examination of realities should not be distorted by the aim to please or inhibited by the risk of displeasure."
--Kingman Brewster

When you take that all-important first step and decide to enroll in a college or university, you are entitled to all the rights and privileges that higher education offers you. Let us examine what those rights are.

First and foremost, you have the right to ask questions when you do not have the answers. It may involve something as simple as a question about a lecture, a test question, the curriculum, the text and supporting materials for the course, your instructor's qualifications, types of tests – are they standardized, or did the instructor create his or her own? – and many more! Moreover, you have the right to request an appointment with your instructor at any time during the semester to discuss your progress and any other concerns you may have. Or you may simply wish to touch base to let him or her know your thoughts about the course. It is essential in a larger class in which it may be more difficult for the professor to remember you. Keep in mind, professors – particularly full-time faculty – have many courses each semester, so it is often a challenge for them to put a face to a name earlier in the semester when they are still getting to know you. The more you can do to make yourself visible via visits during their office hours, the more likely he/she will be able to connect with you. And suppose at the end of the semester, your grade is borderline. In that case, the fact that you reached out to your professor and indicated a willingness to learn the material and improve just might enter his/her decision to give you the benefit of the doubt and the higher grade. As much as we try to implement objective standards in grading, it is still not an exact science at the end of the day, and there will always be a subjective element to it.

The Online Dilemma: Applying to College

Ok, so you like to rant online. At one time or another, we have all felt the need to vent about what's bothering us. Many of us have taken to online discussion boards, Facebook groups, or any of the countless other social media platforms available to us for this purpose. Perhaps your rant took the form of a long diatribe about your political beliefs and your disdain for the opposing political party. Maybe you disparaged an ex-girlfriend or boyfriend, acquaintance, enemy of a friend, etc. Or perhaps you have just become disillusioned – hopefully temporarily – about the state of the world: climate change and global warming, poverty or the national debt, et al. Whatever the case, keep in mind that you have the right to express your political and social opinions online. And public institutions cannot discipline students for expressing their political and social beliefs online. However, there are exceptions to this. According to Zach Greenberg, Program Officer for Individual Rights Defense Program, and the Foundation for Individual Rights in Education: "Speech that isn't protected is narrowly defined. For example, a true threat is defined as those statements where the speaker means to communicate a serious expression of an intent to commit an act of unlawful violence to a particular individual or group of individuals." If that is your intent, not only could you face disciplinary and quite possibly even criminal charges, it will become even more difficult – if not impossible – for you to avoid the scrutiny of background checks when applying for a job. But even if all your posts – or rants – were seemingly innocuous, they can still be used against you.

Let us look at how that may play out. Suppose you apply for admission to a very prestigious college, one in which the requirements are such that only a small fraction of all applicants is accepted. Moreover, one of the criteria for admission happens to be a personal interview with the Admission Committee. You check your email and discover that you have been selected for a personal interview. Imagine the excitement you are feeling, knowing you have a chance to be accepted to your dream college! Interview day is finally here. You give your shoes one last shine and head for the college admissions office. The committee asks you questions about your goals, what contributions you feel you could make to the field, your character, etc. You think the interview has gone well, and you sense that the committee seems enthusiastic about your candidacy. Walking to the parking lot, you feel a sense of relief that you may well have finally made it! All the while, the committee is debriefing and reviewing their notes from your interview. And low and behold, they have determined that you will be one of the two finalists for the position. The committee chair reminds the committee not to consider any information other than what is in the candidate's file: application, resume, personal statement, high school transcripts, etc. This information includes any background information that may be available online. Background checks are under the purview of the Human Resources office.

And so, the committee calls it a day and heads out the door. But it just so happens that curiosity gets the best of one of the committee members. While at home on his laptop while enjoying a good merlot, he decides to google you. We have all felt an urge to google someone at one time or another, right? Maybe it is a friend, a love interest, or perhaps ourselves. Throughout his search of your online records and your social media, he discovers that you have taken an interest in politics. And he is a staunch supporter of candidate A, a candidate who represents all things conservative. You, on the other hand, could not be more opposite. You are a staunch supporter of all things liberal and liberal candidate B. Your online posts reflect that. Upon reading further into your posts, the committee member begins to feel a sharp pain in his stomach. He cannot get over the fact that you would oppose his favorite candidate, Mr. Conservative. It is one thing to support the candidate of your choice; it is quite another to disparage the other side so blatantly. In his mind, you have gone too far. Remember, he was instructed not to search your online records or even to consider any information other than what is in your file. After all, it would be discriminatory, wouldn't it? So, he will just forget that it ever happened and erase it from his memory, right? Because in general, people endeavor to do the right thing, at least most of the time. Perhaps. Or perhaps this information will now become part of his collective unconscious file on you and will be used against you at some point. Maybe he will invent another reason to vote against your application. He may concoct a rationalization that the other finalist simply has more significant potential than you do, and ostensibly, his or her letters of recommendation and personal essay are more beautifully written than yours. In the final analysis, it will be extremely difficult — if not impossible — to prove discrimination on your part. The admissions committee could simply select another finalist for whom the college is a better "fit." But the real reason may be because you alienated a committee member(s) on account of your political beliefs or other views that you posted for all the world to see. So, it benefits you to take extra precautions concerning your social media posts and any additional information you may have out there that could be used against you. As my father used to like to say: "It's hard to get the toothpaste back in the tube."

Keep in mind that private schools can set their own rules about student expression, even how students dress. So, all social media vitriol and invective that you have out there could come back to haunt you. You may want to consider scrubbing your social media accounts, if necessary. It is a process that involves the complete erasure of all content and files. However, there are consequences to this as well, as you may no longer be able to communicate with your employer(s) effectively. If you are a business owner, who relies on social media to generate revenue, it may be counterproductive for you to go this route. In his best-selling book, The Art of Invisibility, Kevin Mitnick, one of the world's most famous hackers, explains the processes and steps to take to be completely invisible on the internet.

Whatever you decide, just be mindful of the pros and cons of having a social media presence and post – or not! – accordingly.

Your Rights on Campus: Decoding the Code of Conduct

Now that you have arrived on campus as a newly minted freshman, ready to immerse yourself in the rigors of academic life at your chosen (hopefully) college, it is time to prepare for your first semester. Your intellectual rights are probably furthest from your mind at this point. Like most college students, your thoughts revolve around your dorm and meeting your new roommate (if applicable), checking out the campus, getting your books, orientation, and preparing for this new chapter of your life. Your college hosted an orientation program before you arrived in which you received voluminous amounts of information about this department and that department. And, of course, the processes and procedures you need to follow when appropriate. You met many people including faculty, your academic advisors, student mentors, and on and on. Does anyone expect you to remember all this information? I certainly hope not. Having been directly involved in many orientation activities for students over the years – either as a presenter, representing my department, a volunteer, or in various other capacities, I have often wondered whether we as a college are disseminating the right amount of information, at the right time to the right audience. Or was it merely just bouncing off one ear and back into the atmosphere? Whatever the case, I am sure that we could do a much better job of apprising students' academic rights and decoding the code of conduct. Before we examine what those rights are, some background on the Student Code of Conduct:

According to findlaw.com (Findlaw 2016), student codes of conduct serve both the classroom and the individual. This document, which is typically found in the college catalog and on the college web page, outlines students' rights and ensures that no student will be penalized or singled out based on anything other than a violation of established rules. It outlines students' responsibilities to ensure that students are aware of the standards they need to meet to ensure their success and that of their class.

Student conduct can encompass a wide range of behaviors that establish the college or university code of rules and regulations. A violation of the student code of conduct could be as simple as failing to return an overdue library book to carrying a concealed weapon into the building. It is up to the college or university administration – often working collaboratively with parents and students – to set its own rules and to enforce them as they see fit.

A standard school code of conduct outlines the rights and responsibilities of both students and faculty. It lists all the various infractions, and they are categorized according to their level of severity. It also prescribes appropriate disciplinary measures, and it explains in noticeably clear terms the student's right to appeal any disciplinary action.

Keep in mind that both students and faculty have rights and responsibilities. Students have the right to be informed of college and university policies and regulations. They also have the right to know the academic requirements for each course they take – this includes grading, attendance, no show and absence policy, course requirements, etc. They also have the right to be advised of their progress regularly. All of this information is part of the syllabus. Unless there is an emergency or extenuating circumstance, you should not have to wait more than 48 hours for a reply to your email or phone call.

Concerning personal property, your possessions are generally off-limits. However, there are always exceptions to this rule. If the college or university believes that you are carrying something illegal, such as a knife or gun, they have the right to search you and confiscate it. Desks and any lockers are school property and can be inspected without your consent or permission.

Faculty have the right to be able to do their job without distractions or interruptions. Therefore, they, too, have the right to discipline students appropriately when it becomes necessary. Most codes of conduct are written with enough flexibility to allow faculty leeway when handing out disciplinary measures. Remember, no one student is above the class. If one student is disrupting the class, it jeopardizes learning for the entire group, all of whom have the right to an education free of distractions in the classroom.

Suppose a student is accused of committing an offense that violates the college or university code of conduct, resulting in a suspension or expulsion. In that case, they have the right to appeal the decision under due process rules of law (Findlaw 2016). No student can be punished based on race, sex, color, religion, disability, or national origin. What if the alleged infraction occurs off college or university grounds? In most cases, college and university jurisdiction applies to actual school grounds. However, codes of conduct are also valid when students attend school-related functions off the existing school property.

Academic Freedom and Academic Standards

As a student in higher learning institutions, you have the right to individual fundamental constitutional freedoms. First and foremost is your freedom of speech, peaceful assembly, petition, and association. If you have a visceral reaction to an event that is happening globally, and you wish to protest in a nonviolent manner, go for it. Care to assemble a group of friends to do the same? Also within your rights. One caveat: your rights end when your protest, petition, etc., disrupt the university's operations, or if it interferes with the rights of others to exercise their constitutional freedoms. Naturally, there are many "grey" areas here as to what constitutes disruption or interference. When in doubt, consult with the dean of students on your respective campus. If you are still not satisfied with his or her answer, you may wish to contact a civil rights attorney. Or better yet, many campuses have an attorney on staff who offers free legal services to students in need.

No matter how "controversial" your views may be – and believe me, in twenty-five plus years of teaching, I have heard a lot of controversial things, some of which do not bear repeating – you have the right to study freely, discuss, investigate, conduct research, or teach. In the classroom, this means that you have the right to state divergent opinions, challenge ideas, and critically examine data or views offered with an open mind. Many students are often reluctant to do this. They simply do not want to make waves for fear of how it may affect their grade or their professor's impression of them. The truth is most professors genuinely appreciate a voice of dissent. Put yourself in their shoes for a moment. Would you want to hang out with a bunch of lackeys for an hour, three times a week, for fifteen weeks? I didn't think so.

When it comes to academic standards, you have every right to know what measures are in place to evaluate your course's academic performance. Faculty are often required to report on measurable learning objectives for their classes. They may be in the form of a standardized report to their department chair. So, if they must be accountable to their bosses, it is only fair that they are responsive to you, the student. After all, if it were not for your enrollment, they would not have the privilege of teaching before you. It is your responsibility to seek clarification of any standard or question at the beginning of the semester. If you wait until the end of the semester when your grade is in jeopardy, you have waited too long. If you have a problem with your grade, talk to your instructor first before utilizing the grade appeal policy. Some students make the mistake of bypassing their instructor and appealing directly to the department chair or dean. Even if you feel like appealing to your instructor would be an exercise in futility, it is still incumbent upon you to follow the proper protocol. If you don't, you will be regarded as someone who circumvented the chain of command. Even if your case is strong, this can be used against you and further serve to alienate your professor. You have the right to be evaluated solely based on your academic merits, without regard to anything related to diversity or conduct unrelated to academic matters. For example, if you wear a t-shirt to a class that reflects your views – which are in contrast to your professor's – this cannot be used against you when evaluating your work. However, he or she can invent another reason for "lowering" your evaluation. But let's give our professor the benefit of the doubt. The overwhelming majority of educators are in this to empower you to be your best self and because they love to teach. Not because they are out to get you. There is no need to be obsequious. Just be mindful of your rights. If you feel your grade is given capriciously, you are accorded protection through the Grade Appeals Procedure outlined in your student Code of Conduct.

Confidentiality

Suppose you have a conflict with your parents, your boyfriend or girlfriend, or another student. Maybe you are not getting along with your roommate either. Whatever the case, you decide to confide in your professor. When you do, keep in mind that you have a right to the confidentiality of information, but it is your responsibility to clearly state what you wish to be confidential or not. There are, of course, exceptions to this rule. Suppose the information you share reveals that you or someone you know is in a life-threatening situation or is in any way a threat to themselves or others. In that case, your professor, counselor, or advisor has a moral and legal obligation to report it. If he or she does not, they could be held liable. Review self-disclosure and confidentiality laws in your state to determine which regulations may be applicable.

Concerning personal safety, you have a right to a classroom free of hazards to safety and security. If you do not feel comfortable on account of a security or safety issue, report it to campus security – and your professor – immediately! Remember, if you see something, say something! And better to err on the side of caution when it comes to your safety. You also have a right to a learning environment free of illegal drugs or alcohol. And you have a right to pursue an education free of disruption or interference. Implicit in this right is the expectation that your professor will enforce acceptable classroom behavior norms. If you are experiencing trouble in your class from another student or students, do not automatically assume that your professor is aware of it. The view – and the perspective – from the other side of the podium is much different than yours. Your professor may be so focused on the class discussion or materials that he or she is not aware of the disruption's severity, or that it is a disruption to you. It is imperative that you advocate for yourself.

You have the right to a classroom in which diversity is welcome. But what does this mean? Colleges are all about diversity. They spend a great deal of time promoting it on their web pages, on social media platforms, across their curriculum, and virtually every professional development day workshop. Professional development days are typically held the week before classes. They are an opportunity for faculty and staff to partake in various continuing education opportunities. You can bet that almost every professional development day features a workshop that's "diversity themed" these days. There is even a section on diversity in two of the courses I currently teach: Career Educational Planning (this class helps students figure out what they want to do and then helps them get there) and First-Year Freshman Seminar. The truth is, I do not spend a lot of time talking about it.

I have always believed that diversity and respect for others regardless of race, religion, creed, color, age, nationality, sex, sexual orientation, or disability start at home. I think you could make a compelling argument that if you have not acquired an appreciation and respect for diversity by the time you get to college, it may be too late. Your views may well be cemented into your psyche by this point. Does that mean one cannot change and become more tolerant of others from different walks of life? Of course not; epiphanies transcend generations! We all, hopefully, have a moment of profound enlightenment at some point in our lives. But I do not believe it is the college's job to force diversity down students' throats. Our job is to set the parameters within our classroom to ensure that all students are respected. However, I do like to engage students with a fun game of Diversity Bingo in which they ask questions about other cultures and customs, among other things. So, I would like to think I am doing my part to celebrate it and promote it. I always want to tell students: "Don't make the mistake of falling into an ethnocentric trap." It is a great big world out there. Explore it. As the title of Thomas Friedman's book suggests, the world is indeed flat!

An often-overlooked academic right concerns intellectual property. You have the right to expect that the materials presented – or distributed – to you in class follow copyright law. Also, you have the right to expect that your creative work will not be disseminated or published without your permission. If you feel that you have an idea or an invention that has the potential to change the world, consult with a patent lawyer. If you receive notification from a faculty member that the information provided in his or her course is the faculty member's intellectual property, do not distribute, use it for creative purposes, or create derivative works without first obtaining the faculty member's express permission. Never assume consent without first receiving written notification. The same rules apply to the intellectual property of other students. And be sure to review your college's statement on plagiarism. Most syllabi these days have a statement that addresses plagiarism and the penalties for engaging in it.

Your Rights Under Title IX

Title IX was implemented in 1972 as part of the Educational Amendments Act, which evolved from the Civil Rights Movement. Its primary aim is to deter colleges from supporting sex discrimination. Title IX states that "No person in the United States shall, based on sex, be excluded from participation in, be denied the benefits of, or be subjected to discrimination under any education program or activity receiving federal financial assistance." Simply stated, Title IX makes it mandatory for educational facilities that receive money from the federal government – this includes colleges and universities – to protect their programs against sex discrimination. Any facility that does not comply with this act will lose their federal funding.

You may be wondering how this act may apply to you. Title IX requires schools to respond to and remedy hostile educational environments, concerning sexual assault, sexual violence, sexual harassment, and bullying which is not limited to physical bullying but also includes cyberbullying, a growing problem among college students. It means that established policies and procedures must be in place to handle these claims. Victims of these crimes are often afraid to come forward for fear of retaliation, not only from the perpetrator but also from the college. The law prohibits colleges from retaliating against you for filing a claim. Nor are they permitted to ignore any retaliatory harassment from other students. So, if you bring a claim or a complaint to the attention of a faculty member, an administrator, or any other person in a position of authority at the college, and they tell you not to worry about it, give it some time – it will blow over;

they would not only violate Title IX, but more than likely enable the perpetrator. If they tell you to consider enrolling elsewhere, that is also in violation of Title IX. The college must provide a remedy and resources to support you while you are at the college. It may involve, at the minimum, counseling and support, medical, and legal services.

If you are under 18 years of age, and therefore still a minor while an incident occurs, the process for filing a claim is much different. Professors, counselors, and administrators are mandatory reporters. It means they are required by law to report any Title IX cases to law enforcement, child protective services, child abuse hotlines, or any other agency for which it may be appropriate. Ultimately, this may lead to a police investigation, making things very unpleasant for the survivors or victims of these crimes. Keep in mind that laws vary from state to state concerning who is a mandatory reporter.

Regardless of age, every college or university has an official Title IX Coordinator responsible for handling a Title IX report's logistics and advocating for your rights if you are a victim of sexual harassment, assault, or bullying. The coordinator will reach out to you. If you are over 18, you are not obligated to respond to your coordinator if you do not feel comfortable doing so. You may wish to consult with your attorney first, which is perfectly acceptable. Do not feel pressured to talk to anyone with whom you do not feel comfortable. Suppose you are a victim, and you decide to speak with the Title IX Coordinator at your college. In that case, the coordinator will discuss your situation and evaluate concrete steps needed to ensure that the remainder of your educational experience is safe. You will have the option of opening an official investigation. If the investigation goes in your favor, the college will have various remedies available. These may include but are not limited to no-contact orders of protection, class schedule changes, and in some cases, even expelling the perpetrator from school. Keep in mind that these investigations are separate from any criminal case you may choose to file with law enforcement. In most circumstances, you are under no obligation to file a claim with law enforcement. If your perpetrator has a long rap sheet filled with a history of assault and abuse, the coordinator may well open an investigation against your wishes. Their rationale for doing so would be to protect the college and other students from repeat offenders. Although their intentions may be fair, this is not necessarily in your best interest. Be aware that there may be people handling your case who have ulterior motives. What is best for the college is not necessarily what is best for you.

You may be thinking, sexual assault or rape is relatively rare, and I probably will not ever have to deal with anything like that. The author John Krakauer in his bestselling book Missoula: Rape and the Justice System in a College Town, states that

"Rape is a much more common crime than most people realize, and women of college age are most frequently the victims. According to a special report issued by the U.S. Department of Justice in December 2014, from 1995 to 2013, females aged 18-24 had the highest rate of rape and sexual assault victimizations compared to females in all other age groups (Author's Note)." Krakauer references another study in his book from the CDC, which focused on sexual violence from a public health perspective rather than criminal justice. The study focused on assaults involving drugs and alcohol. The 2011 CDC study estimated that across all age groups, 19.3 percent of all American women have been raped in their lifetimes, and 1.6 percent of American women reported that they were raped in the 12 months preceding the survey. It accounts for nearly two and a half million people. And it is worth noting that these are reported cases. Likely, the numbers are much higher; it is just that many victims of rape and assault are reluctant to come forward for fear of retaliation.

What if it turned out that the college was working against you, or their interests ran counter to yours? What recourse would you have? As Krakauer points out: "The adjudication process – in rape cases – differs in crucial ways from the way rape cases are handled in the criminal justice system. When a victim reports a rape allegation to college or university administrators, they are likely to have two predominant goals. First, determine the facts as quickly and accurately as possible. Second, if the accused student is found guilty, to protect other students by immediately banishing the rapist from the campus." These goals are similar for other related offenses. "Colleges and universities understand that they have a responsibility to avoid punishing the innocent. However, the harshest penalty a college our university can impose is expulsion. Expulsion does not deprive an accused student of his liberty or give him a criminal record, and most colleges and universities believe the best course of action is to discover the truth than to protect the rights of the innocent at any costs. Because colleges' and universities' adjudications of alleged rapists – and other alleged offenses – are disciplinary proceedings rather than criminal proceedings, the college or university is not bound by the rules of evidence that pertain to the criminal justice system. Therefore, it is free to give as much weight to alleged victims' rights regarding the rights of individuals they have accused. Many colleges attempt to minimize lawyers' roles in handling rape cases to prevent legal wrangling and haggling from obscuring evidence. In the case of the University of Montana, students have a right to have a lawyer present during hearings. Still, the role of the lawyer is limited to consultation with the student only. He or she is not permitted to raise objections, consult with, or speak directly with university officials at any time during the proceedings."

Consider the implications of this. The college or university is obligated under Title IX of the Educational Amendments of 1972 to protect students from sexual harassment and sexual violence, and other related crimes. However, it is conceivable that the college may rush to judgment in its haste to resolve your case, thereby excluding essential facts and evidence that may support your claim. Perhaps they succumb to public and political pressure from powerful donors, alumni, and influential community members to resolve the case quickly and minimize the damage so as not to create a public relations nightmare. After all, treasured full-time enrollments (FTE's) are potentially at stake. Education, as much as we would like it to be all about enlightenment, also happens to be a business—a multimillion-dollar one in many cases. So do not automatically assume that just because you have retained an advocate, who presumably will help you navigate the adjudication process, that everyone is on your side. It is not to say that they are not; it is just a friendly reminder to ensure that your rights are protected, which may run contrary to the college or university's rights. Also, consider that the president of the college typically appoints jurors on college and university courts. The court is a mix of undergraduate students, graduate students, faculty, and staff members. You have a right to know the screening process used to select a jury. It is not inconceivable that the president has, in fact, "stacked the court" to further advance his or her agenda, which may well run contrary to your best interests.

Transgender Student Rights

Title IX rights and protections extend to issues concerning transgender students. State and local statutes, including anti-bullying laws, may apply. At least a dozen states and the District of Columbia have laws prohibiting discrimination based on sexual orientation or gender identity. Following are some examples of how Title IX and related laws protect college and university transgender students.

According to the U.S. Department of Justice and Education, the National Center for Transgender Equality, and the National Education Association: Legal Guidance on Transgender Student's Rights, schools must treat students' gender identity as the student's sex and according to how they identify their gender. It applies even if the student's records or other identification documents (financial aid, transcripts, etc.) indicate a different sex. Schools must not require legal or medical evidence from students as evidence of their gender. In some situations, schools may offer single-sex classes and extracurricular activities. Colleges must allow transgender students to participate consistent with their gender identity. Transgender students have a right to be placed in campus housing according to their gender identity. Students should inquire as to whether their college provides for gender-inclusive housing. Transgender students have the right to use campus restrooms and locker rooms according to their gender identity. However, some schools are exempt from this policy. Title IX prohibits bullying or harassment of transgender students. Schools are obligated to take action to end such bullying once they become aware of it. If a college fails to take reasonable steps to protect a student's privacy relating to gender status, including his or her name or sex assigned at birth, they violate Title IX. Transgender students also have the right to change their educational records regarding their names and gender marker. And if they believe their official college records are inaccurate or misleading in violation of their privacy, they are entitled to a hearing to challenge them. Schools may segregate their athletic teams, but they may not adopt or adhere to requirements that rely on broad generalizations or stereotypes regarding the differences between transgender students and others of the same sex or others "discomfort with transgender students". Furthermore, schools may not discipline a student or exclude him or her from school activities for appearing or behaving in a manner consistent with their gender identity or in a way that does not conform to "stereotypical notions of masculinity or femininity."

If you feel your rights as a transgender student have been violated, here are some steps you can take: First, and most importantly, know that you do indeed have rights as a transgender student. Visit your college's website for information on Title IX and your rights under your school's code of student rights and responsibilities. If these rights are unclear, or if you have questions, do not hesitate to contact your school's Title IX office or office of student affairs to clarify. You may want to prepare a list of questions in advance of the meeting to ensure a response to your questions. If, upon meeting with your college's Title IX Coordinator, you are still not satisfied with the answers, you may wish to consult with an attorney to familiarize yourself with state and local laws. File a complaint with your school if they cannot resolve the problem. Contact the U.S. Department of Education's Office of Civil Rights (OCR). And finally, consult with an attorney to better understand your rights under federal and state law. Most attorneys offer a free consultation.

College Enrollment Contracts

College enrollment contracts exist primarily in the private sector and are the domain of for-profit colleges and universities. Not to be confused with letters of intent, which are typically used by colleges when recruiting athletes. Students applying to and enrolling in colleges receive voluminous amounts of paperwork: applications, financial aid forms, housing forms, orientation forms, and on and on. Some of it is routine, and some can feel very overwhelming. On top of that, they may well have to complete the additional form: enter the enrollment contract.

Enrollment contracts are formal, legal agreements, so naturally, they will include standard language, aka legalese, that may be entirely unfamiliar to the typical undergraduate applicant. Unless, of course, they have had prior legal training. If you are like most traditional – or even nontraditional – age college students, your first inclination is to sign everything as quickly as possible so that you can get on to the business of higher education. However, it is essential to keep in mind that the enrollment contract, unlike your placement test results, housing, or financial aid application, is not put in place to protect your interests. Instead, its primary purpose is to protect the interests of the educational institution for which you are applying. And in doing so, the language in the contract is structured in a way that limits your legal rights should something go wrong.

Let us look at how this can work against you. Suppose you decide to invest your time and your hard-earned money in a college that you believe will position you for a well-paying job. But instead, you end up on the unemployment line with a mountain of debt. You are wondering if you are maybe just an anomaly. After all, there were several hundred – if not thousand – graduates in your class. So, you decide to do some investigating. Maybe you even create a Facebook page for your graduating class.

Upon doing so, you discover that most students have suffered the same fate. They are indeed unemployed, knee-deep in debt, and thoroughly disgusted with the college. The college misled them during the recruitment stages with advertisements promising 100% job placement rates – which should be a red flag to any student. First, no college can "place" a student into a job. Moreover, it is not appropriate for a college to find a student a job. Instead, it is the responsibility of the student to secure gainful employment on his or her own. The college's role – typically under their Career Services Office's auspices – provides career and transition assistance to the student. Services range from career counseling, help with resumes, cover letters, mock interviewing, assisting the student in registering with various job banks (including the campus's homegrown database), and anything else about career planning and placement. But ultimately, it is the responsibility of the student to determine his or her future career path. Any college that guarantees students employment prospects is, at the very least, advertising falsely.

With all this new information at your disposal, you decide to hold the college accountable for their false and misleading advertising. You discover that buried somewhere in the enrollment contract that you signed – undoubtedly while you were enduring the euphoria of beginning this next chapter of your life and thus, not thinking or reading very lucidly — a provision that prevents you from going to court. It reads something like this:

"The mandatory arbitration agreement states that you must take your complaint to an arbitrator — a lawyer chosen and paid for by the college. There will be no chance for depositions before your hearing, no discovery process that might allow your lawyers to uncover any wrongdoing, and essentially no way to appeal the arbitrator's ruling."

Under such a grievance process, there is little doubt which way the arbitrator — remember he or she is on the college payroll — will rule.

In one notable case Debbie Brenner and other former students at Lamson College in Peoria, Illinois, believed they had a slam dunk case against a school that defrauded them. According to The New York Times, the case went to court, but the judge dismissed the case because the students' enrollment contracts that had been signed when they initially enrolled included a "forced arbitration" clause. In forced arbitration, a company requires a consumer or employee, in this case, the student, to submit any dispute that may arise to binding arbitration as a condition of employment or enrollment. The student is then required to waive their right to sue, participate in a class-action lawsuit, or appeal. In arbitration, the former students found themselves making their case before a corporate lawyer who seemed determined to defend the school and for-profit education at any cost. Ultimately, the arbitrator ruled against the former students. To make matters even worse, they socked them with a legal bill of more than $350,000 because of the "hardships" the students had supposedly inflicted on the company that owned the school (Habash and Shireman 2016, 2).

The ways schools use enrollment contracts with restrictive clauses fall into four basic categories:

1. Forced arbitration clauses.   These provisions prohibit current or former students from going to court to seek resolution of any complaints. For example, a student seeking a refund for what they consider an inadequate education would have to take their complaint to an arbitrator in a private binding process. Therefore, it behooves you to know your rights before you consider signing an enrollment contract. You have the right to ask the school about their credentials, independent ratings, curriculum, data from graduate surveys, etc. You may even want to ask to sit in on a class and meet with professors of your choice before you decide to sign anything.

2. Go-it-alone clauses restrict students who have complaints from joining with peers who may have similar complaints against the school (through group or class action). Instead, they must seek

resolution on their own. Therefore, it is incumbent upon you to do your research in advance to determine if any legal claims are pending against them. Of course, the school will probably not be very forthcoming with information, but you may be able to glean a lot from how they respond to your inquiry. Indeed, the truth can be beneath the layer(s) of the answer.

3. Gag clauses prohibit students or former students from telling other people about the complaint resolution process or any final ruling specifics. If the college has a gag clause, then it will be exceedingly difficult, if not impossible, for you to get information about pending or final rulings. Gag clauses would give me pause for that reason alone.

4. And finally, Internal process requirements. All colleges encourage students to make use of internal grievance procedures. Still, these provisions prohibit students from taking their complaints to other forums for resolution without first going through the school's internal process. There may well be exceptions to this rule if one's life is in danger. Again, you as a student have the right to clarify what, if any, exceptions apply. Moreover, it is a good idea to get these exceptions in writing to have documentation should you need it sometime down the road.

Proponents of enrollment contracts argue that they provide consumer protections against frivolous lawsuits as well as an expeditious resolution of grievances. But at the end of the day, they become a license for dishonest and predatory behavior and a check on students' rights. They run counter to one of the necessary foundations of higher education: to provide a forum for critical thinking and a laboratory to examine ideas without fear of reprisals. As Kingman Brewster once said: "Universities should be safe havens where ruthless examination of realities should not distort by the aim to please or inhibited by the risk of displeasure." Enrollment contracts do not encourage this "ruthless examination of reality." Nor do they put students' interests first. Instead, they create a breeding ground for unscrupulous marketing and lower-quality education. Buyer beware!

Bullying on Campus

At one time, bullying was just something that took place on a playground, a school cafeteria, or maybe a locker room. Many people believed that it was merely a grade school issue. Those days are long gone. The reality is that bullying is not limited to grade school, and its reach extends to colleges and even the workplace. Unfortunately, cyberbullying is a growing problem that has proved to be a formidable challenge to colleges and universities. According to a 2013 study entitled Bullying

Victimization Among College Students: Negative Consequences for Alcohol Use, by Kathleen Rospenda, Judith Richman, Jennifer Wolff, and Larisa Burke (Rich 2019) it is indicated that among a survey population of 2118 college freshman, 43% experienced bullying at school, and 33% at work. Bullying falls into three main categories:

Physical – This typically involves physical violence, property destruction, theft, forced consumption of alcohol and drugs, and sexual assault.
Verbal – In addition to name-calling, it can include taunting, intimidation, and threats.
Social/Relational – This involves harming victims through relationships and reputation. It can include exclusion, spreading rumors, revealing secrets and fears, and public mocking.

In recent years, due mainly to the increasingly widespread use of social media and technological advancements in smartphones, cyberbullying has emerged as a significant issue that colleges must now address. Cyberbullying can lead to physical violence and combines aspects of verbal and social bullying to harm victims. It could involve spreading sensitive information or images about victims online, cyberstalking, targeted harassment, threats of harm, exploitation, humiliation, and most recently, "doxing." Doxing occurs when a bully publicly posts a victim's personal contact information to encourage harassment. Revenge porn is another particularly extreme form of cyberbullying. It involves distributing or posting sexually explicit materials of the victim online. These could include private messages, videos, and text messages.

In a high-profile 2010 cyberbullying incident, a Rutgers University student Dharun Ravi secretly recorded and publicly posted a video of his roommate, Tyler Clementi, kissing another man in his dorm. Shortly after Clementi reported the incident to a resident assistant and school officials, he jumped to his death from the George Washington Bridge. This tragedy reinforced just how real an impact cyberbullying can have. The Clementi case also shined a light on how bullying can intensify in a college setting. For most students, college is a time of discovery, a coming of age, and a time when one's identity starts to take shape. But college campuses can also be confining, more so for students who are away from home for the first time. And if bullying occurs on campus near a student's campus residency, it can make it difficult to retreat. The victim may feel lonely and isolated, being away from his or her support system back home.

Bullying can also occur in student clubs and organizations. Although these groups will support and bring students together, they may lead to power imbalances, abuse, and exclusion, which often lead to withdrawal from day-to-day life. There are serious short- and long-term effects on victims. These may include depression, anxiety, PTSD, as well as a decline in physical health. Also, college students risk a decrease in academic achievement, and are far more likely to drop out of school.

The Clery Act

If you are the victim of bullying, you have rights under Title IX and the Clery Act. Both offer protection against sexual harassment, bullying, discrimination, and assault. The regulations state that your college or university has a legal obligation to act on claims related to these behaviors.

The Clery Act was passed in 1990 and named after a Lehigh University student murdered in her dorm room in 1989 (Boston Globe 2012). It protects students by forcing schools to be transparent about campus crime. Under this act, college administrators must report all criminal allegations made to them in good faith, founded on more than rumor or gossip, to a designated campus official. That official is then required to submit a tally of the allegations to the federal Department of Education. The department publishes statistics each year for every school in the country that receives federal financial aid. The act also requires schools to keep thorough crime records and to show them openly. Although it does not require administrators to report allegations directly to police, it does require them to offer to help victims to do so, an important distinction.

Specifically, the Clery Act requires all colleges and universities that receive federal funding to disseminate a public annual security report (ASR) to employees and students every October 1st. If you are a college student, you may recall receiving notification of this report's availability in your inbox around that time of the year. The ASR must include statistics on campus crime for the preceding 3 calendar years, and it must consist of details about efforts taken to improve campus safety. ASR must also include policy statements regarding (but not limited to) crime reporting, campus facility security and access, law enforcement authority, the incidence of alcohol and drug use, and the prevention of/response to sexual assault, domestic or dating violence, and stalking (Clery Center 2018).

Not only are college administrators required to report criminal allegations to a designated campus official, but all institutional officials with significant responsibility for campus and student activities are required to do so. This group includes but is not limited to: faculty who serve in an advising capacity to students or student groups, coaches, and staff involved in student affairs. Only professional mental health and pastoral counselors are exempt from reporting when acting in these roles (Vanderbilt University 2020).

Suppose a student reports an incident to a Campus Safety Official in confidence. The official documents the Daily Crime Log incident and the statistic in the Annual Security Report. So even if the incident is reported anonymously (without revealing the victim's identity) through a campus security official, the college is required to record the nature of the incident and the approximate time and location to ensure accuracy.

Arrest vs. Conviction

Under the Clery Act, a person does not have to be convicted of a crime before it is reportable. An important implication of this is that it leaves open the possibility that someone could be wrongfully accused and then must clear their name. Thus, it may discourage some students from coming forward. The bottom line is, if you see something, say something. It is always best to document and err on the side of more communication rather than less if you feel you have witnessed a crime.

Institutions are required to report crimes committed on campus grounds and geographical locations that include buildings and properties owned or controlled by the institution that are reasonably contiguous to one another and directly support or relate to the institution's educational purposes. Also, buildings or properties that fall within the campus, are reasonably adjacent to it, that the college owns but does not control; students frequently use it to support the institution's educational purposes (Vanderbilt University 2020).

If you reside in a residential facility, this is a subset of the on-campus category. This may include the following types of housing:
Undergraduate, graduate, and married student housing.

- Single-family houses for student housing.
- Summer school student housing.
- Buildings used for student housing and have faculty, staff, or any other individuals living there.
- Buildings owned by a third party that have a written agreement with the institution to provide student housing. It does not matter whether the rent is paid to the institution's third party on behalf of the students or paid directly.
- Housing for officially and not officially recognized student groups, including fraternity or sorority houses, that are owned or controlled by the college or located on property that the college owns and controls.
- Public property refers to property owned by a public entity, such as a state or city government. It includes thoroughfares, streets, sidewalks, and parking facilities within the campus or immediately adjacent to and accessible.

- Any building or property owned or controlled by a student organization that the institution officially recognizes; or
- Any building or property owned or controlled by the institution used in direct support of or with the institution's educational purposes is frequently used by students and is not within the institution's same reasonable contiguous geographic area.

Source:police.vanderbilt.edu/crimeinfo/cleryactfaq

Student Housing

I have always felt that college is the most exciting time of one's life. It is a time of independence, coming of age, and making new friends and connections. However, to have a happy and healthy time, it is essential to have acceptable living conditions and be aware of your rights as a tenant, whether in a college dormitory or off-campus housing. Bear in mind that living in a dorm room is different from a standard landlord-tenant arrangement. But even though living in a dorm room is different, students living in dorms still have certain rights. One such right is an implied warranty of habitability (Findlaw 2020). A warrant of habitability is indicated in all rental housing, whether it is an apartment or a dorm room. This warranty guarantees that the tenant's dorm room or housing unit:

- Is not infested with bugs or rodents.
- Has hot and cold running water and heating, if necessary.
- Has a proper, safe, and secure lock on all doors and windows.
- Is sealed off from the elements.

The Warranty

There is an implied promise in nearly all 50 states, read into residential leases, that the property will be suitable for its desired purpose. For renters, this means that space will be ideal for inhabiting. Also implicit in this promise is that the landlord will maintain substantial compliance with any applicable building codes and make repairs as necessary. The point of the warranty is not to oppress the landlord by forcing exact compliance with all regulations. It only requires substantial compliance, which means minor or temporary issues will not amount to a breach of the warranty, nor will they excuse the renter from paying full rent. Implied warranty of habitability dictates that slumlords shall not profit from maintaining an uninhabitable property. Many slumlords are acutely aware that college students often lack the financial resources to contest such deplorable living conditions, or they simply do not know the law and become victims of exploitative rental policies.

If you feel an apartment or dormitory's condition falls below the minimum required by the local building code, there are a few remedies. First, carefully document the item(s) in need of repair and take photos of all areas in question. Then submit a request for repairs to the landlord or, if applicable, to the student housing office. If the landlord, or college, refuses to make repairs, you could consider reporting them to your local building inspector. Just search building inspectors in your area for contact information. As a last resort, you could withhold rent. A portion of the rent, equal to the apartment's diminution in value, should be placed into a separate bank account. If the tenant paid the full amount of rent, they might recover part of the paid rent as overpayment due to the violations. If the landlord attempts to evict the tenant on account of nonpayment or partial payment withheld, the code violations will serve as the tenant's defense. Keep in mind; this is the last resort. It is always best to carefully document the issue and attempt to resolve it with the landlord first. Of course, it is best to consult with an attorney before deciding to take that final step.

Most college and university housing departments have a system in place for reporting problems with your dorm room. Refer to your college's website for information regarding how to report a problem or complaint. When it comes to student housing, students tend to have fewer rights than students who choose to live off-campus. Specifically, they have fewer rights concerning privacy. In an apartment, a landlord has to give notice before entering a tenant's apartment. Also, the tenant would have to have a valid and specific reason for entering the apartment (Findlaw 2020). However, in student-run housing, the amount of privacy a student has depends mainly on the college's housing policy. So, it would serve you well to familiarize yourself with your school's housing policy. And ask questions and advocate for yourself! That is, after all, the whole point of this book: to empower you to advocate for yourself. For example, you may want to ask what, specifically, is the policy about entering the dormitory? Ask to see it in writing in the school's housing policy manual or wherever such language appears in the student handbook.

Right to Fair Housing

Fair housing means that everyone in the U.S. has a right to choose an accommodation free from unlawful discrimination (Findlaw 2020). Federal, state, and local fair housing laws protect people from discrimination during housing transactions such as renting a house, apartment, or condominium.

Fair Housing laws prohibit discrimination against certain protected classes. The protected types as defined by the Fair Housing Act (Findlaw 2020) include race, color, national origin, religion, disability, sex, and family status. State and local fair housing laws can also offer even more coverage to include age, marital status, and sexual orientation.

Although students are not a protected class in themselves, they are still protected and have rights under fair housing laws. Students have the right to ask about, apply for, and obtain housing without being discriminated against on account of their race, religion, national origin, color, disability, sex, family status, or any other protected class status given to them by state or local laws.

Discrimination can be tough to prove on your part. As in the example I cited earlier in this book of the student who is passed over for college admission ostensibly because she is less qualified, you, too, can be passed over for a variety of reasons a landlord chooses to invent, none of which are free from discrimination. Unfortunately, that is the reality of housing today. If you are a student who feels you have been discriminated against while looking for or applying for student housing, you do have options. You can file a complaint online with the U.S. Department of Housing and Urban Development (HUD). You can also contact your local HUD office for further information. Right about now, you are probably thinking, jeez, that is just going to be one big morass of a website filled with bureaucratic red tape. It will take forever and a day for me to fill out the requisite "complaint" forms with no guarantee that an actual human being will even receive it, let alone read and act on it. Well, do not despair; there are plenty of fine folks at HUD and elsewhere who want to help you. If they do not respond to your complaint immediately, do follow up and advocate for yourself.

Dealing with Campus Police

Many college students have questions about campus police officers' role and their rights, should they have an encounter with campus police. As is the case with any police encounter, you have the right to remain silent, and you are not required to answer any questions. Your Fifth Amendment rights protect you from making any self-incriminating statements. And be advised that "anything you say can and may be used against you in a court of law" before you decide to speak when questioned by police.

Your Miranda Rights entitle you to have an attorney or lawyer present while being questioned when in custody. Attorneys know the law and understand what questions police officers can ask and what you can answer. Hence, it is always an acceptable policy to contact one before answering any questions that may incriminate you. And keep in mind that every county has a Public Defender's office with attorneys that serve the public when they cannot afford a private attorney. According to Austen Erblat (2013), in the state of Florida, officers are required to ask these two questions:

Do you understand each of these rights I have
explained to you?
Having these rights in mind, do you wish to talk to
us now?

Remember, an officer cannot arrest you for
not talking to him or her! If the officer tries to
pressure you into talking, but you do not feel
comfortable doing so without an attorney present,
stand your ground. You do not want to self-
incriminate yourself. It is easy to misspeak or have
your statement misinterpreted or incorrectly stated
by police in their report. Think like a text message
that you just fired off to a friend you regret ever
sending. The Fourth Amendment protects citizens
from illegal search and seizure. If a campus police
officer asks if he or she can search your car, you can
always say that you do not consent to the search. It
may not stop them, but he or she must then find
probable cause or reasonable suspicion that you are
committing – or are about to commit – a crime.
Probable cause could include observing someone
who is – or appears to be – intoxicated, certain odors
such as alcohol or marijuana, or anything in plain
sight (alcohol bottle, roach, plastic bag, or weapons).

Concerning dorm searches, every college is
different. Even if there is nothing in your Housing and
Residential Life Guidebook or housing contract
stating that police have the right to search your dorm
room, that does not mean that they can't enter it.

Dormitories are college or university property, which is often sufficient justification for campus police to enter without a search warrant. However, college or university staff must typically give 24-hour notice before searching your room. Keep in mind that the threshold for probable cause to search is relatively high. The mere smell of marijuana smoke under someone's door is not sufficient probable cause. Sufficient reason would only be present if there were evidence of a violent act in progress. Otherwise, the police cannot merely ask the RA to let them into your dorm room. Without explicit consent or a warrant, any contraband found cannot be used against you in a criminal investigation. It could, however, still result in disciplinary action by the college or university.

If you are stopped for suspicion of DUI whether by campus police, municipal police, or state police, some of the same rules apply. You do not have to submit to a breathalyzer test. In many jurisdictions, you do not even have to step out of your car to do a "field sobriety test" (College Post 2020). However, in nearly all jurisdictions, that will result in a suspension of your license for up to 90 days.

All police officers are required to inform you if you are being placed under arrest, being detained, or are free to go. When stopped, you are absolutely within your rights to ascertain which of the three applies.

Although there are some similarities to being arrested, whether you are a college student or any other adult, it can also be different in many ways. There are programs to help if arrested for DUI as a first-time offender. You do not have to consent to a search of your person unless you are under arrest. And police need a search warrant to search your vehicle. If the police stop you, you must provide your license, registration, and proof of insurance. However, you do not need to say where you are coming from and where you are going. Students – and many adults – often feel pressured to disclose this information, but the fact of the matter is that it is none of their business where you are going or from where you came.

Who has the authority to arrest you? It does not matter whether the police on your campus are merely security guards or officers of the campus police force. All have the authority to arrest you. If your arrest is imminent, prepare in advance, if possible. More than likely, you will not have access to your cell phone, so memorize your family's or your lawyer's phone numbers. And formulate an emergency plan if you have children that need to be attended to or take medications. When arrested, the police must inform you of your Miranda rights, that is, "you have a right to remain silent." And you would be wise to follow that advice and not talk without an attorney present. This practice applies whether you are on or off campus.

By now, you have probably watched enough Netflix movies to know about the technique known as good cop/bad cop, the psychological tactic used by police to try to get you to be more forthcoming with information. While in custody, campus police officers might try to "buddy-up" and act like your friend to get you to reveal information that may well end up incriminating you. And some may try to bully you into revealing information that may make you appear guilty in court, even if you are innocent of all charges brought against you!

So, about that "phone call." You have the right to make a local phone call. Police are not allowed to listen if you call your lawyer – but they can listen to calls made to anyone else. So be cautious if speaking to family or a friend while in their presence.

If Campus Police Violate Your Rights

First, do not resist arrest or a search to which you have consented. Even if police violate your rights, it is still a crime to physically resist an officer, whether it is a campus police officer or any other jurisdiction. Second, it is of paramount importance that you document everything you can. Ask officers for their names and get their badge and car numbers. And be sure to record everything as it happens using your phone camera. Remember, you have a legal right to record anything and everything if you do not interfere in police work or present a danger. Be sure to get the names of all witnesses and contact them as soon as possible to obtain their statements. Document, document, document!!

After the college or university administration's violation, take your "documented" complaint as high up the chain of command as you can. It means to the college or university president's office, if necessary. Often, lower-level administrators want nothing more than to bury an issue to save them any additional headaches. However, you have the right to due process, and if it makes them uncomfortable, that is their problem, not yours.

Finally, if you feel you have exhausted all options and have no other resources at your disposal, tell media outlets your story. There is nothing like the power of bad publicity to dissuade a college or university administration from pursuing a case unless it is justified.

Remember, campus police do not wield the power of God or whatever deity you may follow. Their primary purpose is to protect you, and they must respect your rights when carrying out their duties. As a college student, you have rights that cannot be taken away from you – by campus police, college or university administrations, or anybody else.

Financial Aid Advocacy

Navigating the complexities of college aid can be a daunting task. If you are not familiar with financial aid terminology, award letters can be tough to read. Each school's letter can look different and can be chock full of ambiguous terms and unexplained costs. It is a bit like trying to understand all the closing costs on that first house you are purchasing. Thus, financial literacy and the ability to advocate for your financial needs have become an essential part of the college application process.

In a June 2018 study, New America published a financial aid report that stressed the need for greater transparency in financial aid award letters (Apple 2019). The primary findings revealed that not only is financial aid often insufficient in meeting students' needs, but award letters themselves are confusing to the average student or parent. As a result, it has made it extremely difficult for students and parents to understand just how much college will cost. Moreover, this convoluted process and lack of consistency have made it difficult to compare costs of attendance across colleges.

When it comes to borrowing money, be an informed consumer and do your due diligence and research. Once you have done so, you will be more prepared to advocate for yourself in the financial aid office of your chosen school. Keep in mind that schools allow students to negotiate their financial aid packages by providing more information and compelling evidence that their financial need is more significant than what was initially determined. Remember, everything – including your financial aid – is negotiable!

Becoming fluent in the language of financial literacy has additional benefits. There are plenty of other reasons to connect with your financial aid office. For example, most schools have an emergency aid fund to help you with temporary financial emergencies. These may include housing problems, food assistance, and gap funding between payment of financial assistance periods. Remember, you may never know about these resources unless you ask. And in this context, asking is equivalent to advocating.

Furthermore, your financial situation – or your parents' – may well change. You are required to reach out to the financial aid office, explain all changes to your financial situation and why that warrants an increase in aid, if appropriate. They cannot read your mind and will not come to you. You need to take the initiative on your own.

There are also lots of grants and scholarships available in the private sector. The United States Department of Labor offers a free scholarship search tool. A basic search of scholarships and grants available to college students will provide further resources you may want to utilize. Remember, scholarship applications will not arrive on your doorstep courtesy of your Amazon delivery driver — although it would be nice if they did, wouldn't it? — you must put in the time and effort and conduct a thorough search of all scholarships for which you may be qualified. And if you are borderline in terms of meeting the qualifications for applying, go for it anyway. What do you have to lose, not even a postage stamp anymore? You never know who else may — or may not — have applied for it at the time you did. If the applicant pool is weaker, this will work in your favor.

When I was applying to graduate programs, I recalled reading about available graduate assistantships at Edinboro University. I reviewed the qualifications, and my first thought was, "I'll never get one of these." My grades were ok, but surely there would be plenty of students with more impressive credentials lining up to apply. But the other part of me thought, "why not, what do I have to lose?" If I recall correctly, the postage on my application amounted to close to $1.00. So yes, I did lose that dollar. But the loss was well worth it when, to my surprise, I received a letter from the admissions office confirming that I had received an all-expense-paid graduate assistantship, including a tuition waiver. You never know … so go ahead and go for it! Advocate for yourself!!

Part of learning the language of financial aid involves learning how to detect scholarship and financial aid scams. Unfortunately, they are out there waiting to pounce on vulnerable and gullible applicants. Be wary of high-pressure sales tactics often employed at so-called financial aid seminars that require you to pay immediately or risk losing out on the opportunity.

Some companies guarantee that they can get scholarships on behalf of students or award them "scholarships" in exchange for an advance fee upfront. These same companies offer what they claim to be a "money-back guarantee." Read the conditions attached to that guarantee very carefully. They often attach conditions that make it impossible to collect the refund. It is relatively easy to hand over your money, during which time everyone may seem so friendly, but it is often much harder to get it back. Some provide almost nothing for the student's advance fee, not even a list of sources, and others may tell students that they are "finalists" for awards that require an upfront fee. If you have not figured it out, by now, the "upfront fee" is code for a scam! Some companies are even so bold as to ask for a student's checking account number to "confirm eligibility," then they debit it without the student's consent. Other companies quote a relatively small "monthly" or "weekly" fee and then ask for authorization to debit your checking account – for an undetermined length of time.

Other companies claim they have programs that could make you eligible to receive financial aid, including grants, loans, and work-study. For a processing fee, they will handle all the paperwork. If you encounter any of these companies, run far away from them! The application that determines eligibility for programs is the Free Application for Federal Student Aid (FAFSA). You can complete and submit this form for free. (Source: Federal Trade Commission consumer.ftc.gov)

According to the FTC (2020) these are some additional lines that should be red flags for you:

- The scholarship is guaranteed or your money back.
- You just cannot get this information anywhere else.
- I just need your credit card or bank account number to hold this scholarship.
- We will do all the work. You just pay a processing fee.
- The scholarship will cost some money.
- You have been selected by a "national foundation" to receive a scholarship – or "You're a finalist" in a contest you never entered.

If you choose to attend a financial aid seminar, take your time, and do not feel pressured into signing anything with which you are not comfortable, or seminars that pressure you to buy now or risk losing the opportunity. Advocacy skills come into play here. Investigate the organization. Check with a counselor or financial aid advisor before you decide to spend your money. Often, you can get the same help for free. Be very wary of success stories or testimonials of extraordinary success – the seminar operation may well have paid "shills" to give glowing reviews and testimonials. Kind of like reading an online review. Do you ever wonder if the company merely paid the person who wrote that review to boost their ratings? How would you ever know that they were not? Exactly – so be extra cautious of the so-called glowing review. Instead, ask for a list of at least three local families who have used the service in the last year. Then follow up with those families to see if they are satisfied with the products and services received. If they are unable to provide a list of families, then that should be another red flag.

Finally, ask what the total charge is for the service, the services performed, and the companies' refund policy. Get the refund policy in writing! Keep in mind that you may never be able to recoup the money you give to an unscrupulous operator, despite the stated refund policies. You certainly do not want to be expending unnecessary time and energy chasing down a refund that you may never see, not to mention all the stress this will cause you and your family.

PART 3

CREATING AN ADVOCACY ACTION PLAN FOR CAMPUS LIFE

"If I am not for myself, then who will be for me? If I am only for myself, then what am I? If not now, when?"
-Hillel the Elder

What Is Engagement? Show Me the Advocacy

To engage and advocate, you must figure out what is important to you and discover who you are. If things do not matter to you, or if you do not value them, you probably will not be inclined to advocate for them. Equally as important, you must determine who you are not. Figuring out who you are not often comes first. I have always felt that figuring out who you are not is very underrated. As a career counselor with over 25 years' experience in higher education, I have worked with many undecided students over the years. I cannot tell you how many times I have heard students say, "I don't know what I want to do." Invariably, I would ask them what they do not want to do. Sometimes I would get a blank stare in response to the question, but most of the time it would generate a lengthy discussion and brainstorming session. At the very least, it is a starting point for inquiry, which often leads to new ideas, possibilities, and exploration.

For most college students, figuring out who you are and what you value the most is no easy task. It takes a considerable amount of time, reflection, and research. You must be willing to be vulnerable and step out of your comfort zone and thoroughly explore all possibilities. Ultimately, there is no guarantee that you will find all the answers. Let us be honest; some people sail through life wondering, what if I did this or that? And then they wake up one day with regrets. Or, perhaps life became more complicated, and thus, it became harder to pursue their dreams. Do not be that person. You have a golden opportunity here. Seize the moment!

To help you with this process, I suggest beginning with a simple values clarification. The following is a list of values. Review the list and select the top ten values that are most important to you and rank them from 1-10, with 1 being the most important:

Love		Adventure	
Money		Variety	
Family		Freedom	
Ethics		Recognition	
Knowledge		Popularity	
Power		Independence	
Friends		Humor	
Free Time		Loyalty	
Beauty		World Peace	
Stability		Spirituality	
Respect		Fairness	
Reason		Creativity	
Safety		Achievement	

Now that you have identified what is most important to you, the next step is to clarify your values and determine how you will translate them into action and goals. The left-hand column identifies the values you defined earlier, in rank order from one to ten. In the next column, remember the purpose you have associated with that value, and in the third column, determine a plan for what you are going to do about it. In other words, how will you advocate for yourself?

	My Value	Goal What do I want to happen?	How am I going to advocate for it?
1.			
2.			
3.			
4.			
5.			
6.			
7.			
8.			
9.			
10.			

For example, if your top value is an achievement, perhaps one of your goals would be to become more well-rounded while in college. Maybe you see yourself getting more involved in college activities outside of the classroom. You will advocate for this by taking the initiative, joining a few student clubs, and engaging in more student activities. Maybe you value competence, and thus, your goal is to be more competent in a particular skill at work or school. Your plan of action to address this goal might involve taking a continuing education course or additional course work in your specialty area. Equally important, you may set a goal to learn to accept fallibility and the mistaken notion that you must be perfect at everything. In turn, you acknowledge that being perfectly imperfect is ok. Whatever the case, identify what is important to you, determine what you want to happen, plan, and go after it! You will not regret it!

Build Your Advocacy Portfolio: Financial Aid, Curriculum, and Community Advocacy

Everything Is Negotiable!

Let's face it; college is not going to get any cheaper anytime soon. Given the climbing price tag, a financial aid package or scholarship offer can be the difference between a yes or a no when enrolling in college. If your aid package is not what you had hoped it would be – and you feel you deserve more, or your circumstances have changed – ask for more money. The Free Application for Federal Student Aid (FAFSA) can be filed as early as October 1. The early filing date allows colleges to send out financial aid award letters sooner, so you have even more time to file an appeal before the May 1st national deadline for tuition deposits. According to Northwest Mutual (2020), there are four concrete steps you can take on the road to financial aid advocacy:

1. Ask for a Specific Number: With respect to financial aid, do the math. If you apply to more than one school, determine each school's net cost on your list. The net worth would be the total price of attendance (including tuition, room and board, books, food, and transportation) minus any scholarships and grants. Then calculate what your family can afford to contribute and compare

it with each financial aid award letter. The gap between each award will be your sweet spot.

2. Put Your Appeal in Writing: Many students and parents make the mistake of just showing up unannounced to the financial aid office. It would be akin to just calling their office, and the first thing out of your mouth is something like "I need to make a change to my financial aid form" before you even get to hello. Remember, people — especially financial people — appreciate context. So, it is best first to identify yourself and why you are calling. The same goes for showing up unannounced. It will not get you very far. They will need to sit down and carefully review your paperwork before rendering a decision. It does not happen on the spot, especially not when you show up without prior notice. Furthermore, the person you make initial contact with probably does not have the power to change your offer. Even if they could, it's not done on the spot. Most schools have an appeals protocol or professional judgment that you must follow to appeal. Review your schools' protocol before you file an appeal. If you cannot find it online, give them a call. Typically, you will need to fill out a form and attach a cover letter with documentation. Appeals usually fall under one of two categories: need-based or merit-based. Need-based requests look at exceptional circumstances not indicated on your FAFSA. These may include unforeseen medical bills, the loss of a parent's job, an income reduction, or extra expenses for elderly patient

care and divorce or separation. If you incurred expenses from a natural disaster, that could also qualify you for further need-based financial aid. If your academic record (grades and test scores) has dramatically improved, you may wish to make a merit-based appeal, or if a similarly ranked school offered more in merit scholarships or grants. If that is the case, go back to your top choice and use the better award as leverage to ask for additional money. Indicate in your appeal that you will enroll if they can match the offer from your competitor. Provide Evidence for Everything: Be as detailed and thorough as possible. For need-based aid appeals, include every fact, date, and figure about your current financial situation, and provide supporting documentation to justify any claims of hardship. That includes things like receipts, medical bills, official termination letters, bank statements, etc. If you are negotiating for additional merit-based aid, attach copies of award letters from competing schools to show the college the costs they are up against and how much is needed to close the gap. Include proof of improved test scores and grades and any letters of recommendation.   As   for   letters   of recommendation, I highly recommend you have a minimum of three at your disposal, preferably from people who can speak to your abilities, aptitude, and qualifications, both personally and professionally. If you have closer to five or six references, even better. Why only meet the minimum requirement? Why not go above and beyond that? It certainly cannot hurt you to have an extra authority or two, nor is it an imposition on the financial aid office to have them in your file. All these things can move you further up in the school's rankings, thus making you a more attractive candidate.

3. Reaffirm Your Interest: Another mistake students make during the financial aid process – or in a job interview for that matter – is to fail to reaffirm their interest or commitment. They automatically assume that the school will gauge their interest level just because they have applied to the school. Not necessarily. Communicate to the school that they are in fact, your top choice. We all feel better when we are wanted. Make it known that just a little bit of extra aid can turn the tide in the decision to enroll. Also, be sure to thank the school for the package they have put together. Never underestimate the power of a simple thank you! It does wonders sometimes. Explain to the school that you are willing to take on your responsibility based on what you can realistically budget and take on in loans. Most of the time, when an appeal is approved, it is a relatively small offer, about $2,000 - $3,000 for that year. Colleges certainly do not have the financial means to fund every student they have accepted. Don't take it personally if you fall short of your target number.

4. Finally, mail or email your letters to the appropriate offices. Need-based aid appeals go to the financial aid office. Merit scholarship

negotiations usually go to admissions or enrollment offices. Be sure to follow up within a week with a phone call, or better yet, make an appointment for an in-person visit. It is always better to go face to face when it is possible.

Whether or not your appeal(s) is successful, you will feel good about advocating for yourself. If it is not successful, do not despair. You can always reapply the following year.

Other Ways to Get Involved

Every year the President submits a formal budget proposal to congress detailing federal spending priorities. It may mean more spending for the military and national security and less for domestic and international aid programs, or vice versa, depending on which party is in power. Regardless, there are several concrete steps you can take to advocate for financial aid:

Write or Visit Your Representative. Write your representative a personalized letter or email, or better yet, do both. It gives you more name recognition. Remember, representatives receive vast amounts of mail, both paper and electronic, so the more you can do to make yourself stand out, the better your chances of getting their attention. Your representative or senator's website will list addresses for their Washington D.C office and local district offices, and they will have an online form to contact them via email.

Whenever you are back in your hometown or plan to be in Washington D.C., plan to visit your representative's office and share your experiences in person. I recommend you call and make an appointment to speak with the staff, rather than dropping by unannounced. When you contact their office, you can request to make an appointment to talk directly with your representative rather than their team. You will probably end up speaking with their staff, but that is ok. Practice advocacy!

Unless they have been living under a rock for the past twenty years, nearly all representatives have Twitter, Facebook, and Instagram accounts which provide a forum for you to share your experience and ask them to support financial aid programs in the budget.

And remember, the more you can personalize your message, the better your chances of moving the needle. When thinking about what to share with your representatives, consider addressing the following questions:

Why did you decide to go to college?
Are you a first-generation college student?
Why did you choose the college you are attending?
What are your post-graduation goals?

Which financial aid programs do you depend on
and why?
How has financial aid impacted your college
experience?
How are you making the world a better place by
attending college?

In my view, higher education is the single
most important investment you can make in your
future, and investing in higher education is a
partnership between students, institutions, and the
government. Whether you are for big government or
not, the fact is government has always played a key
role in investing in our future generation of leaders
and innovators. So, share your story and help your
representatives understand the direct impact cuts in
financial aid programs have on their constituents.

Classroom Advocacy

Whether you are in the traditional brick-and-
mortar classroom or the virtual classroom, there are
plenty of ways to practice self-advocacy. If you have
an Individualized Education Plan (IEP), be prepared
to explain it to your professor in your own words. It
is conceivable that your IEP may be interpreted
differently by your professor than you intended it to
be. Words alone cannot defend themselves without
a voice attached to them. Be that advocate and be
that voice! Email your professor a copy of your IEP
file to explain what specific accommodations you will

need. Then follow up with an appointment for further discussion or to clarify and answer any questions they may have.

Learn to make modifications on your own. If something is not working for you, change it! That could be something as simple as increasing the font size of a word document, using a screen reader, or sitting a bit closer to the front of the room so that you will be more inclined to pay attention. If you do not feel like your IEP is being adhered to properly, initiate a conversation with your professor and ensure that it is. Remember, silence is consent. If you do nothing, you are merely endorsing a learning environment that does not meet your needs. You are a paying customer, so you are entitled to a return on your all-important investment.

Concerning tests, curriculum content, syllabus, and textbooks, you have an active role to play! Do not just accept the test at face value, especially if it is not standardized. Ask the professor how he or she created it. How did he or she ensure that it is not only reliable but also valid? These are rather important questions that deserve answers. Quite frankly, if a student asked me this about my tests, I am not sure how I would answer. I was not happy with the "standardized" tests offered in the textbook nor the tests used in our department for one of my courses. So, I decided to create my own tests, complete and fill in the blank, instead of the default multiple-choice tests. My evaluations have been good over the years, and based on student feedback, most students seem to be receptive to the tests, and the grade distributions have reflected this. They are, in fact, consistent with the norms for similar classes. Yet, the question would probably still make me a bit uncomfortable. But as far as I am concerned, it is not such a bad idea to make professors uncomfortable sometimes. Making someone uncomfortable can often be the first step towards greater accountability. Personally, I welcome the opportunity to be put on the spot and taken out of my comfort zone if the result is that it leads to greater accountability and provides students with an opportunity to advocate for themselves. Sometimes we (faculty) lose sight of why we are here in the first place. It is not because we like to hear ourselves talk – although, for some in this arena, that seems to be the main incentive – instead, it is to serve students, prepare them for the world of work, educate them, and empower them to be their best selves!

The same goes for the textbook. Some questions to consider: Ask the professor why he or she chose it? Why was it selected over other texts? How is it going to be used? Will it supplement lectures? Does the professor have a particular area of expertise? Will test questions come from the book, or lectures, or both? One more than the other? How often has the book been updated? Be advised that college textbook updates and revisions are usually of minimal significance – sometimes, only a single paragraph – and they are often updated so that the author can receive a residual payment for the update without really having to update much of anything. Sound like a racket? Absolutely.

As for the curriculum and syllabus, if I were a student, I would ask the following questions: How is the grading scale used? If I am between grades, will consideration be given to give me the higher one? How do office hours work? Can I drop by, or do I need an appointment? Is it better to call or email my professor? Remember, everyone is different in this area. Some professors, like many students, are incessant texters and emailers, while others prefer face-to-face interaction. Find out what your professor prefers and adjust accordingly. One exception: if you have vital information to share concerning grades, paperwork, or other necessary documentation that would support your case and your status, always submit it in writing first. That is your protection to ensure that it is received. Copy yourself on the email and keep a copy of it! Then, follow up with a face-to-face meeting. I cannot tell you how many times I have had a student say, "I sent you this or I sent you that," and my reply is always "well, if you sent it when you claim to have sent it, then simply forward me a copy of the original email and I'll give you credit for it." If they sent it, then they should have a record of it. Unless, of course, they deleted it. When it gets to me, I can always verify the original submission date and time. People lose stuff, so keep careful records.

Read your syllabus carefully. It is, after all, your learning contract. If you have other questions about the schedule, textbook, supplemental texts, or learning activities, ask! One more note about office hours. Make it a point to check in periodically and ask how you are doing in the course, and what else, if anything, you can do to improve your standing. It is easy to become invisible, especially if the professor has a full course load and all his or her classes are large lecture classes, and they are all maxed out. If this is the case, making yourself more visible will almost certainly work to your advantage.

Finally, recognize when you need to ask for help. If you are in doubt, take a step back, assess the situation, and consult with a close confidant or advisor. Even though the heart of this book is about encouraging you to advocate for yourself, I am acutely aware that sometimes there are problems that we just cannot solve on our own. Surround yourself with a good support network of family, friends, faculty, and student support staff who can step in to assist you when it is needed.

Community Advocacy – Using Social Media

Whether you reside on campus or commute to college, you will never be more than a few clicks away from a direct link to community advocacy. Check with the Student Activities Office on your campus. They most likely have clubs or organizations that promote community advocacy. Getting involved in community advocacy is a great way to sharpen your advocacy skills and become an agent for change on your campus.

If you decide to get involved in your community, there are plenty of ways to use social media to unite your cause. First and foremost, it will provide a common platform to share stories. It will also provide for quick turnaround time, enable you to raise funds quickly, and unite large groups of people around a common cause. And it will encourage solidarity.

Be advised that there is also a downside to social media activism. Some hashtags are overused – and even trolled – to the point that it can become difficult to hear an emerging organization over all the noise. Unless, of course, they are lucky enough to catch the attention of a celebrity and end up going viral.

From an individual's perspective, social media does not necessarily encourage conversation about an issue because all the algorithms show users content based on what they like. People end up living in, or gravitating to, a bubble that only echoes their thoughts. Indeed, hearing what we want to hear is a desirable proposition. Therefore, it is difficult for an organization to reach out to non-supporters to convince them of their cause. That does not mean you should discount it entirely. There are still plenty of good examples of how to use social media to your advantage.

One example of a successful social media advocacy campaign is the "Post It Forward" campaign launched by Tumblr in 2015 (Narayanan 2020). The aim of launching "Post It Forward" was to break down the silos of cyberbullying, body shaming, and issues related to sexuality. People shared their personal stories and struggles without the fear of being judged. Individuals facing emotional or psychological distress could engage in a positive conversation and find the support they needed. The hashtag #PostItForward made it easy to connect users directly to support and counseling resources and find other stories.

The "Post It Forward" campaign generated attention. Some VIPs like President Joe Biden and celebrities like Brittany Snow, Pete Wentz, Jordin Sparks, Elizabeth Banks, Wendy Williams, and the First Lady of New York City Chirlane McCray supported it. They helped jump-start the conversation by sharing their own stories and advice.

In addition to going viral on Tumblr, it also went viral on leading social platforms such as Instagram, YouTube, and Twitter. Using GIFs made the campaign popular among younger college-age audiences, who happened to be their target segment.

Think of the implications of this for you as a college student. Make your campaign discoverable through eye-catching #hashtags and use graphic art and quick-witted content to gain attention. Utilize GIFs so that college students can relate to it; you have the potential to organize an advocacy movement not only on your campus but perhaps regionally, nationally, and even internationally. Indeed, you are only a few clicks away from changing your life and changing the world for the better.

Leveraging Future Employability Through Advocacy - Why You are in The Game!

So why advocate? What is in it for you? There are numerous benefits to being an advocate during your college years and beyond, not just in terms of personal growth but also professionally. When you advocate for yourself or for a cause you believe in, you cannot help but raise your profile and enhance your qualifications for prospective employers. If you start now, you will slowly but surely begin to develop a record of service that distinguishes you from other candidates with whom you may one day be competing. You will enhance your resume and LinkedIn profile – two critical pieces of your job search portfolio. Equally important, you will feel a great sense of personal pride, achievement, and accomplishment.

You will begin to establish connections, build partnerships, and forge valuable alliances – in some cases invaluable – with experts in their respective fields. It will undoubtedly add to your knowledge base. Thus, you will become much more well-rounded, yet another advantage in today's job market. Remember, you do not "get" an education; you must make one for yourself. It is not just about the transcript and the degree. When you step out of your comfort zone and add to your vault of knowledge, that's when real learning takes place.

You will help give your college and community recognition. You will be developing valuable organizational skills that will serve you well throughout your college years. Advocacy may even help you narrow down your career choices if you are still deciding on a major. When you advocate, you gather information about different career fields and provide support to help you make choices. It could even present an opportunity for job shadowing with a prospective employer.

When you advocate for yourself, be sure to document it and keep a journal. Whether it is something as simple as requesting additional test time or questioning a test question and persuading the professor to discard it, maintain detailed records of what you did and when. These accomplishments will come in handy when you begin to build your resume and when you have to answer what separates you from other candidates in a job interview.

Ultimately, advocacy helps you to get people to understand your point of view and vice versa. It makes it easier for you to obtain information in a way that is understandable and relatable. It opens doors in terms of showing you what other services are available. It will provide you with a platform for self-expression. You will have the privilege of representing your college or community and empowering people to work towards solving problems. If not now, when?

PART 4

BONUS FOR PARENTS! ENRICHING THE CAMPUS EXPERIENCE FROM A PARENT'S PERSPECTIVE

"When the learner is ready, the teacher will appear."
-Chinese Proverb

What is Parental Advocacy?

When it comes to the best way to parent our kids, we all think we are experts, right? Or at least those of us who are parents. There is no one size fits all approach that will work for every parent and every student, and it would be very presumptuous of me to tell you how to parent. After all, I know less than nothing – and that is not much – about your children. I will, however, share with you some tips for parenting college students that I think have merit. Equally important, some suggestions for what not to do. As someone much wiser than me once said: "Sometimes we have to figure out who we are not before we can figure out who we are."

Parenting a college student presents a formidable challenge. I would argue there is something inherently wrong with that phrase: "Parenting a college student." By the time your son or daughter makes it to college, it is time to start thinking of the term parenting in more passive rather than active terms. Presumably, you have put in your hard yards. Whether you have been a working parent all your life, a stay-at-home parent, or perhaps both like me, you have been engaged and involved in your children's lives, and hopefully, that has promoted optimal development. But it is now time to pass the torch.

Ok then, so what should I do to be the best parent I can be? While advocating for them, liberating your children does not mean abandoning the warm emotional bond you have created. Continue to maintain a friendly, emotional, and loving bond with your children. We have all heard that either from the latest Instagram or Facebook post, self-help parenting book you have just read, or maybe it is written somewhere on the hallmark card you just bought. It probably sounds like empty platitudes by now. Nevertheless, I believe its importance is far too often very underrated. So, engage in constant communication with your children. Ask questions about their day and positive and negative experiences; if they wish to answer your questions and engage, great. If not, that is fine too, but do not force it if they are not ready to. The more you push, the more they will push back.

Expressing love for your children does not always have to be an active process. You can still love them from afar. Wherever you are, bear in mind that you can never have too much love and warmth in a relationship, no matter how old your children are!

Of course, every child is unique, and every child brings unique gifts and challenges to the table. Sometimes we need to be more involved in helping our children navigate the challenges of college. And sometimes, we can more easily let go of the reins. If you are the parent of more than one child, you know all too well that what works with one may not work with the other(s). So, do not take your cues from other parents, Monday morning quarterbacks, or any other people who insist on dispensing unsolicited advice. Take your cues from your child, and when all else fails, follow your gut, and do what is developmentally appropriate for him or her.

Make it a point to be involved. Be engaged. But do not go overboard. Before you decide to help, ask yourself if it is indeed a situation that requires your help. Are you helping your child because it will make you feel less anxious, or will it serve his or her best interests? If your child is in imminent danger or distress, of course, you will intervene – that is a no-brainer. But if your college student is experiencing a typical daily hassle, it is best to let him or her handle it on their own. If you do, your child will be learning valuable – invaluable, really – problem-solving skills.

Resist the urge to do things for your child. Instead, offer coaching, support, and encouragement. Many college students are ill-equipped to handle challenging and stressful events, especially since some may be new issues to them. But that is more reason to offer them support and coaching, to enable them to solve the problem(s) independently. And remember, it is human nature – especially among men – to want to problem solve. All too often, people – and that includes your children – just want to be heard without judgment. They often need a sounding board, a shoulder to cry on, or space to vent. Many times the solution to the problem is not to offer a solution! I realize this may sound counterintuitive to many people, but before you pass judgment, practice it. Practice just listening and suspending judgment. You may even wish to offer encouragement and brainstorm solutions with them. Remember, there is a difference between brainstorming solutions and active problem solving! Each time you defer or refrain from doing things for your child, you create a foundation for them built on advocacy and critical thinking skills to provide them with the tools and resources to handle any crisis that comes their way.

It will be tempting to feel as if you want to save your child from everything. Accept that your child will experience some bumps along the road during his or her college career, and that you cannot possibly protect your child from every failure. Even if you could, what good would it do? It would only set them up for future losses because they would never develop critical coping skills and build resiliency.

Think about the long term. You could make a compelling argument that your child would be better off in the short term if you continuously shield him or her from any harmful or stressful events. But if you do, they will never have developed the all-important problem solving skills needed to succeed in the long term. They may be ill-equipped to self-advocate when a situation warrants it. Please give them a foundation built upon autonomy, independence, critical thinking skills, and self-advocacy. The rest will take care of itself.

Understand You Through and Through

If you have made it this far, you probably have a good understanding of what it means to be a parental advocate for your college-age child(ren). But, in order to fully understand and appreciate parental advocacy in action, you must first understand what drives you. As Stephen Covey states in his book Seven Habits of Highly Effective People, "Seek first to understand, then to be understood." In the context of parental advocacy, you must understand the psychology that drives your parenting style. Perhaps you were raised in a family in which your parents were overly involved in your life. Maybe they were very controlling and watched over you like a hawk. Did you feel suffocated and, thus, rebel at every turn? Perhaps you are transferring this parenting style onto your children? Many of the traits we project onto our children result from our own life experiences and upbringing. We are what we know! It does not necessarily follow that you would heed your child's tendencies if you were raised by controlling parents. Maybe it turns out that you take the opposite approach. Regardless, you must understand your history and your motivation behind how you parent before you can begin to implement a parental advocacy plan.

Conversely, you may have grown up in a household in which you had free reign. Did it feel as if your parents were always away, busy, etc., and never around? Therefore, you had to make all the important decisions on your own. Now consequently, do you err on the side of complete disengagement and give your children free rein? Does it feel as if you are interfering with their lives if you engage in the decision-making process? Maybe they feel as if they do not have guidance from you, but you are oblivious to it, because again, we are what we know. And what you know is to let go and disconnect, thereby giving your children the free reign you had growing up.

Often, the consequence of both extreme styles is that your children never really develop the tools they need to make crucial decisions and advocate for themselves. They feel ill-equipped to navigate the complexities of college life. So, what then is the happy medium? I will share my thoughts on what I think is ideal for parental advocacy for resilient and resourceful children. First, let us explore some of the different parenting styles and the challenges associated with each one:

Helicopter Parenting

If you have teenage children, you have probably heard this term in conversation by now, in a discussion thread, or on your favorite blog or podcast. Helicopter parenting is hovering over your children – like a helicopter – at every turn. It can begin with toddlers by preventing every minor fall or avoiding age-appropriate tasks (Gill 2019). A helicopter parent may declare: "I am determined not to let my child ever get a scratch on her knee!" If your child makes it through childhood without ever incurring a scratch, you may be the only parent on the planet who achieves this feat. And props to you if you do! For the rest of us, this is an unrealistic goal.

Helicopter parenting for toddlers may include:
- Speaking with school administrators to make sure their child has a particular teacher perceived as the best.
- Choosing a child's friends for them.
- Enrolling them in activities without their input, e.g., sports, extracurricular, etc.

- Completing homework and school projects for your child.
- Refusing to let your child solve problems on their own.

In the teen years and beyond, this may involve:
- Not allowing your child to make age-appropriate decisions.
- Becoming overly involved in their academic work and extracurricular activities to shield them from failure or disappointment.
- Contacting their college professor about low grades.
- Intervening in disagreements with their friends, co-workers, or employer.

Source: What is Helicopter Parenting? (Higuera 2019)

A helicopter parent may stand over a teenager's shoulder as they do their homework or shadow a younger child each time they ride their bike. Don't assume that helicopter parenting only affects teenagers and college students; it can begin at a much earlier age and continue well into adulthood.

From a parent's perspective, sometimes the root cause is fear about their child's future. They believe that what their child does today has a profound impact on their end, and they believe helicoptering is a way to prevent struggles later in life. Other times, anxiety is the driving force behind it. Some parents become very anxious and fall apart emotionally when they see their child hurt or disappointed, so they do everything to prevent this from happening. Enter the helicopter. In some cases, their identity revolves around their children's accomplishments. Indeed, some parents live vicariously through their children, and their children's success makes them feel validated and like a better parent. It could be that the helicopter parent never felt loved or protected by their parents, so they made it a point never to let their children feel this way. It is certainly normal to have this feeling. Perhaps it would be abnormal if you did not, right? Consequently, this drives some parents to go overboard and give their children an excessive amount of attention. Finally, it could be peer pressure that led to the revving of the helicopter blades. Maybe you feel as if you are lagging behind other parents in terms of accomplishments, and you think you need to overcompensate for it.

Is there any benefit to helicopter parenting? To be fair, there may well be, but it is primarily to the parent. Some research has suggested that helicopter parents enjoy greater happiness and meaning in their lives. (Higuera 2019) This benefit does not trickle down to the children of helicopter parents. Ultimately, it can lead to other problems in children, including more significant anxiety and depression. Unfortunately, these feelings do not automatically disappear when children grow older.   One 2014 study (Gill 2019) evaluating the impact of this style on college students found that students raised by so-called helicopter parents were more likely to be on medication for anxiety and depression. There is also a risk of a child developing entitlement issues, where they believe they deserve certain privileges from having been accustomed to always getting what they want growing up, and so, they think the world should – and will – bend over backward for them. It can result in a rude awakening and a painful reality check for them later in life.

Still, some children act out or become hostile when they feel their parents are exercising too much control over their lives. They may grow up with poor coping skills. They never really learn how to deal with failure or disappointment during their elementary, high school, or college years. And they may lack conflict resolution skills.

If you are a parent and you identify with this style, there are some concrete steps you can take to avoid helicopter parenting and encourage independence (Higueral 2019):

- Rather than focus on the present, think about the possible long-term effects of helicopter parenting. Ask yourself, do I want my child to always rely on me to fix things, or do I want them to develop life skills?

- If your children are old enough to do something for themselves, let them!
- After your child disagrees with a friend, co-worker, or boss, do not get involved or try to fix it. Teach them the skills to resolve the conflict on their own.
- Allow your child to fail. Getting cut from the team or not getting into the college of their choice teaches them coping skills.
- Teach them life skills: cooking, cleaning, laundry, face-to-face interaction, and how to talk with their teachers.

That last point, in my view, is very underrated. It has been my experience that many college students today simply lack communication and advocacy skills when interacting with their professors. As a result, all too often they choose to remain silent. And their silence becomes consent to whatever directive the professor decides to implement, whether it is in the student's best interests or not. Not a good recipe for success. When in doubt, talk it out!

Snowplow Parenting

Snowplow parenting refers to the parents who, like a snowplow, literally remove all obstacles from their children's paths. Although snowplow parenting is similar in many ways to helicopter parenting, there is a difference. Snowplow parents take things a bit further in that they insert themselves into the decision-making process and take the initiative to resolve all their children's issues independently.

Indeed, snowplow parenting can often take things to extremes. Some examples of snowplow parenting in action (English 2013):

At Boston University, one father was so upset over his daughter's A-minus final grade that he called the professor to complain, and then the department chair, and then he even took it upon himself to contact the academic dean! Imagine if, God forbid, she had received a B +. Maybe he would have gotten his state senator involved at that point! A helicopter parent can transition into a snowplow parent. Perhaps that is what happened here.

In another case, a student recalled interviewing for a summer job while his mother stood outside listening to the conversation. She even knocked on the door during the interview and asked to come in! Not surprisingly, the employer did not hire the applicant for the job.

Eleanor Green, a Boston restaurateur, has had similar experiences with these parents (English 2012).

"We see snowplow parents when they come in with their son or daughter to apply for a job." Green's family owns several restaurants, including West on Centre in West Roxbury, MA. "They say things like, 'I am here with my son, Mark, to apply for a busboy position. Mark is standing there in silence. If Mark cannot talk to us, we are thinking, how can he interact with our staff and customers!"

According to Holly Schiffrin, a psychology professor at The University of Mary Washington in Fredericksburg, VA, people need three necessary skills to be happy: they need to feel independent, competent, and able to form and maintain relationships with others. All three of these skills are negatively affected by overly involved parents, aka snowplow parents.

Other examples of snowplow parenting include parents who are on the phone seven or eight times a day with their college kids, or they inundate them with texts all day long to the point where the kids need to turn off their phones or put them on silent to have enough peace and privacy to do their work.

Aubrey Ireland represents an extreme case of parental over-involvement. In 2012, Ireland, a college senior, won a protective order against her parents for stalking and harassing her. Ireland, who was 21 at the time, told a Cincinnati judge that her parents often drove 600 miles from their home in Kansas to the College-Conservatory of Music at the University of Cincinnati, unannounced, to meet with college officials. They then falsely accused her of promiscuity, drug use, and mental problems.

Her parents, Julie and David Ireland, admitted in court that they even installed monitoring software on their daughter's laptop and cellphone! They explained to the judge that they had her best interests at heart. "She's an only child who was catered to all her life by loving parents," her mother explained to the judge.

I do not doubt that these parents genuinely believed they had their daughter's best interests at heart. And maybe their parents snow plowed them as children, so they were merely repeating this pattern of behavior, and that was all that they knew.

I think Donna Pincus, a psychologist at Boston University, sums it up best: "Sometimes, kids need to feel the snow." By enabling our college-aged children to feel the snow, we send a message that we have confidence in them that they know how to navigate their way through life.

Fortunately, most colleges now offer parent orientations, which take place simultaneously but separate from student orientations. The sessions focus on what their children can expect and how parents can support their children best without going overboard. Colleges have written policies for dealing with calls and intrusions from anxious or angry parents. Federal law prohibits colleges and universities from disclosing information about students who are 18 and older without their consent.

As a parent and someone who has spent over a quarter of a century in higher education, specifically in student services as an administrator and adjunct faculty member, I have experienced many of the same kinds of stories when dealing with parents. Some have been, shall we say, a bit over the top in their approach, and that is putting it kindly; others disconnect from their children's lives. The truth of the matter is, when I decided to embark on a career in student services, my thought was I want to get into this business first and foremost to serve students. Quite frankly, the fact that I would have more interactions with parents if I chose to be, say, a high school or elementary school teacher did not appeal to me. It motivated me to steer clear of those careers. The idea of working in a college with minimal interaction seemed like a much better fit for me. It is not that I dislike parents – remember, I am one – I just feel that college is the time for students to blaze their path, sans parents' involvement.

Before you flood my inbox, remember I am not suggesting that you ignore your children. On the contrary, whatever parenting style you feel works best for you – and it is not my place to judge as I do not believe there is any one 'right' or 'wrong' approach – you need to support your kids and make sure they have the information they need to make informed decisions. But remember, sometimes you must allow them to fail, or else they will never be prepared to deal with the larger problems all of us have to deal with in life. Failure is often success in disguise!

The Uninvolved or Neglectful Parent

Uninvolved parenting – sometimes referred to as neglectful parenting – is a parenting style in which parents do not respond to their children's needs beyond the basics of food, clothing, and shelter. (Higuera 2019) Children of uninvolved parents receive little guidance, discipline, and nurturing from their parents. They are often left to raise themselves and make significant decisions on their own. This style is essentially the opposite of the helicopter or snowplow parent.

As you may imagine, it is not without controversy, and thus, for many people, it is easy to pass judgment on these parents. Regardless of whether you are overly involved or under-involved, it is essential to remember that parenting style –

much like any other – is not always intentional. All too often, we automatically assume that it is. Let us consider reasons why a parent may be disconnected or uninvolved. First and foremost, this style may be the result of being raised by neglectful parents themselves. Remember, we are what we knew growing up. Perhaps the parent is dealing with mental health issues that prevent them from forming a type of emotional attachment. This issue may well carry over into the parent's relationship with their spouse or other family members. Regardless of the underlying reason, it is possible to change a parenting style if you become aware of uninvolved parenting characteristics and are willing to address them.

Let us look at some of the tell-tale signs of uninvolved parenting (Higuera 2019, page):

1. They are self-absorbed. Whether it is work, social life apart from kids, or other interests or problems, uninvolved parents are preoccupied with their own affairs. They are unresponsive – or nonresponsive – to their children's needs, and they make little if any time for them. Everything in their life comes before the kids. In some cases, parents might outright neglect or even reject their children. Think of the parent who has no idea where their kids are, what is going on at their college or university, what their day to day lives look like, when they have doctor appointments, etc. If they are in the same room with their

children, they may spend the whole time staring at their phones, not even bothering to look up to acknowledge their existence.

2. Lack of an emotional attachment. For most parents, forming an emotional connection with their children comes naturally. For an uninvolved parent, the bond is not instinctual, nor is it automatic. This parent feels disconnected or even estranged, which severely limits the amount of affection and nurturing they can extend to their child.

3. Lack of Interest in a child's activities. Because of the lack of affection, uninvolved parents are not interested in their child's schoolwork, activities, or events. They might even skip their sports activities, recitals, parent-teacher conferences, etc.

4. No set rules or expectations for behavior. Uninvolved parents typically lack a discipline style. So, unless a child's behavior affects them, these parents do not usually offer any type of correction or behavior modification. They allow the child to act how they want. These parents do not get upset if their child performs poorly in school or with other activities.

Uninvolved parenting can manifest itself in many ways depending on the child(ren)'s age and can begin as early as infancy and extend into adulthood.

In the infancy stage, some parents use all opportunities to nurture and offer affection. However, uninvolved parents may feel disengaged or detached from their baby. They may not be interested in holding, feeding, or playing with the baby and may often find themselves passing the baby to their partner or a grandparent. With young children, an uninvolved parent may show little interest in designs or drawings that the child creates, or they may simply ignore the child as they talk excitedly about their day. They may also fail to make reasonable limits with things like bedtime or cell phone use.

Uninvolved parents of older children may not impose any consequences, or react, or even care if they skip school or bring home bad grades. It is in stark contrast to an authoritarian parent, who will be extremely strict and punish the child that steps out of line.

Balance Reaching Out with Keeping Out

Regardless of which style of parenting you feel is best for your college-age children, you will face many challenges along the way. If your child is attending college far away from home, your challenge will be to stay connected without smothering your child or interfering too much with their day-to-day life. Indeed, it can be quite a balancing act. There are times when you may feel you are overreaching and intruding, and other times when you feel like you can never get your son or daughter on the phone. Perhaps you attempt a phone call, only to be relegated to your child's voice mail, in favor of the dreaded text. Conversely, you lead with the text and get a phone call in return, which may well seem like an imposition on your time if you are an uninvolved parent.

If you are like me in that you endeavor to avoid text on account of its superficial nature, but your son or daughter insists on texting anyway, I say go with it. In my view, it is always best to meet people on their level. There will be a time and a place to engage in a real conversation, aka face to face or via a phone call, facetime, zoom meeting, etc. And if you feel your child is drifting or withdrawing, do not hesitate to take the initiative and initiate conversation. When in doubt, reach out!

Earlier in my career, I often made the mistake of switching the medium. What I mean by that is, sometimes I would receive a call from a student and I would respond with an email, or vice versa, a student would email me and I would pick up the phone. Much like when I was a waiter many years ago, I would often talk to the people who just wanted to be left alone, and when I came across people eager to engage in conversation I would plead the

5th. Ah, communication. It can take a lifetime to master it! Do not despair if it feels like you just are not on the same sheet of music with your son or daughter. We are all works in progress in that regard, and it can take time to adjust to their new lifestyle and the changes that go with it.

Mental Health Challenges Facing Today's Parents and their Children.

I would be remiss if I did not devote some time to addressing mental health challenges in this book. Recognizing them will continue to be of paramount importance going forward. I have identified five of the most common mental health challenges students face in college (Best Colleges 2020): Depression, Eating Disorders, Anxiety, Addiction, and Suicide. Let us explore each one in more detail:

Depression

Unfortunately, depression is a growing problem on college and university campuses today. As I write this, we are still knee-deep in a worldwide pandemic which has undoubtedly caused isolation and depression for many people worldwide. It has caused an increase in documented cases of depression on college campuses. Moreover, most campuses have resorted to online learning until it is safe to return to the classroom. For many students, this has exacerbated feelings of loneliness, isolation, and depression.

I can attest to this, having had my classes converted to online learning last semester. Although I received favorable reviews for my online courses, and many students indicated that my class was their favorite class and the only class they enjoyed logging on to – it still felt like something was missing. I even had one student tell me that my class was the only class in which nobody blacked out their screen. I guess that is the ultimate compliment! But I still did not feel the same level of connection that I know I would have felt if we were face to face. I have always been a face-to-face kind of guy. As someone who has studied communication, I understand the value of creating a presence in a classroom. That is not to say it is all about style and no substance, but with today's student, you better have both, or you will lose them very quickly. As the saying goes: "Who you are shouts so loudly in my ear, that I cannot hear what you say."

Symptoms of depression differ from person to person. Ultimately, depression is the result of a chemical imbalance in our brains. The way one person presents symptoms and signs is not necessarily the way symptoms emerge in others. According to the American Psychological Association, symptoms of depression include, but are not limited to, the following: Changes in sleep habits or appetites, sadness, feelings of being overwhelmed, feelings of hopelessness and feelings of powerlessness, seeing a glass half empty, trouble paying attention, difficulty reading or completing work tasks.

It is not uncommon for students to avoid talking about things that bother them. They may feel insecure, fearful of standing out, or embarrassed. Peers can easily misdiagnose one another, which can often make things even worse. If you observe these symptoms in your child, it is best to refer them to a mental health professional without delay. Unfortunately, there is still a stigmatism attached to mental health counseling today. Many people feel as if they will be ostracized or perceive it as a sign of weakness if they seek mental health counselors' services. Do not fall into that trap. It is perfectly ok to seek out these services. To be clear, we all must endure the vicissitudes of life, and it can feel overwhelming at times. But that is ok. Don't feel ashamed. Remember, most colleges and universities have counseling services available to students free of charge. So, take advantage of this valuable – invaluable really – resource, if need be.

Anxiety

We all experience anxiety from time to time. Sometimes it gets to the point that persistent feelings of worry linger. In that case, tension and panic begin to interfere with daily life, crossing the line, and it becomes a clinical medical condition. As a parental advocate, it is essential to remember that our children's anxiety disorders can sometimes be mistaken for everyday stress or written off as someone worrying too much. Symptoms for anxiety include feelings of stress and apprehension, shortness of breath, irritability, irregular heartbeat, trouble concentrating, muscle pain and tension, fearfulness, and headaches.

The exact causes of anxiety are not fully understood, but they may very well include a combination of genetics, naturally occurring brain chemicals, life experience, and stress. In other words, a little bit of everything. If you feel as if your child is presenting any of these symptoms, reach out. Your child's campus counseling center should have treatment options and resources available to help.

Suicide

Mental health professionals define suicidal ideations as a prevalent pattern of thinking about or planning one's death. In general, experts consider suicidal thoughts as a mental health crisis. If your son or daughter has expressed thoughts about suicide, please take it seriously. And always err on the side of caution. Do not assume that they are merely thoughts and that they will not go beyond that. It is better to be overly cautious than to be too complacent and be wrong. The Association of

American Universities reports that 20% of American college students reported suicidal ideations in 2018 (Best Colleges 2020). News articles from 2019 revealed that suicide rates among young Americans were at their highest ever levels. It speaks to a crisis that extends far beyond college and university campuses' confines and into society.

Signs of suicidal ideation can vary from person to person, but common warning signs can appear in a person's speech, mood, or behavior. Suicidal people may talk about feeling trapped, feeling like they are a burden to others, feeling like they have no reason to go on, and ending their lives. If you suspect your child may be suicidal, contact your campus counseling center immediately.

According to the Anxiety and Depression Association of America (AADA), there are five steps to take if you know someone who is suicidal:

Ask them directly: "Are you considering killing yourself?" Although it may seem rather direct, it does not increase the likelihood of suicidal thoughts, and it is an essential first step.

Make safety a priority. If they answer positively to step one, ask them if they have a plan. It may not be easy but removing lethal objects and items in the dorm or home, such as guns, can also make a big difference.

Be there for them. Sometimes the most you can do for someone is to be there for them when they need you. Being there for someone does not necessarily mean literally, although that would be preferable if possible. Regardless, listen to what they have to say, and acknowledge and talk to them about the realities of suicide.

Give them the tools to help themselves. Save the National Suicide Prevention Lifeline number on your phone: (800) 273-8255. If possible, save it to a friend's phone too.

Remain in contact. Staying in touch makes an enormous difference and can potentially save the life of an at-risk person.

Eating Disorders

Eating disorders cover various conditions marked by irregularities in eating habits and an intense preoccupation with one's body image and shape. Disorders can involve both food deprivation and binge eating, which may be followed by purging. A 2018 study from the National Eating Disorders Association reported that 10-20% of female college students have an eating disorder, and that rate continues to rise. Male students experience lower incidences, around 4-10%, according to the study.

As defined by the National Association of Anorexia Nervosa and Associated Disorders (ANAD), common eating disorders include the following:

Anorexia Nervosa. An unhealthy fixation on thinness, a distorted body image, and fears of gaining weight. This disorder most commonly results in emaciation.

Bulimia Nervosa. Bulimia Nervosa is a binge eating disorder characterized by recurrent and frequent episodes of eating enormous amounts of food, followed by behavior that compensates for it, like purging, fasting, or over-exercising.

Binge Eating Disorder. Binge eating disorder is constant cravings that can occur any time of the day or night. It is often associated with poor body image or low self-esteem.

The signs and symptoms of eating disorders vary from person to person and condition. They are often dependent on the mental state of the individual with the illness. However, several red flags are common factors for anorexia, bulimia, and binging. They include distorted or low body image, dehydration, irregular heartbeat, excessive exercise, feeling like eating is out of control, fear of eating in public, and continually making excuses for eating habits.

Many college students do not seek treatment for eating disorders or are unaware that they have even developed a problem. They can be life-threatening issues and can contribute to these health problems if not treated properly: kidney failure, stunted growth, failure in the reproductive system, heart problems, and menstruation loss.

As the parent of a college-age child, be mindful of these signs and do not hesitate to advocate for your son or daughter if need be. We all have days where our self-image is not the best, and a few bad days does not necessarily signal a problem. But when random complaints about weight become all a person can focus on, or when they start skipping meals or binging on junk food, it is time to act.

Addiction

If you are a parent of a college-age kid, you know all too well that many college students frequently use alcohol and recreational drugs, which can become problematic. Addiction describes a definite pattern of physical and psychological dependence on one or more substances, including intense cravings and indulgence in substance abuse despite known risks and harms. According to a 2019 study regarding addiction on college campuses (Best Colleges 2019), alcohol is a primary factor in 1,500 annual deaths on college campuses, while 35% of students admit to binge drinking and 25% abuse stimulants to enhance studying. College students also abuse drugs like marijuana, ecstasy, benzodiazepines, cocaine, and prescription painkillers at increasingly higher rates.

Although many students who partake in drug and alcohol use in college do not develop addictions, they may still feel the side effects of withdrawal or prolonged use of these substances. Some of these symptoms include slurred speech, bloodshot eyes, impaired coordination, fear, anxiety, or paranoia for no apparent reason, deterioration of physical appearances, such as weight loss or gain, changes in personal grooming, and a developed tolerance for alcohol and drug use. It results in the user needing more of the substance to obtain the same effect, being prone to suspicious behaviors, frequently getting into fights or trouble with the law, having a sudden change in friends or activities, and having a sudden need for money or a financial crisis.

If you are a parent of a college-age child who you believe may have an addiction, there are some questions you can ask to help ascertain whether or not they indeed have an addiction:

- Do they drink to relieve stress or suppress issues?
- Has their drinking or drug use interfered with their relationships with others?

- Have they withdrawn from activities or schoolwork?
- Does their life revolve around drug or alcohol use?
- Have they developed a personality change?
- Have you noticed an unusual smell on their breath, body, or clothing?

If your son or daughter is attending college away from home, it will be more challenging to ascertain whether or not they have developed an addiction. So, if you suspect there might be an addiction in play, try to communicate visually as much as possible – via zoom, facetime, etc. – so that you can at least observe any nonverbal clues and signals they may be putting out.

When in doubt, consult your healthcare provider and the college counseling office for treatment options. Remember, college counseling services are an integral part of student services. They are here to help you and your college-age children. The Substance Abuse and Mental Health Service Administration (SAMHSA) is an agency within the Department of Health that improves behavioral health in the United States. They provide information and a treatment locator by zip code. SAMHSA's national hotline (800) 662-4357 is available 24/7, 365 days a year for individuals dealing with substance abuse.

What Parenting Style Works Best and Why?

Regardless of which parenting style you gravitate to, there are pros and cons to all of them. If you identify with the idea of helicoptering or snow plowing, you may bond better with your children and become better friends. You will probably always know what is going on in your children's lives without your children feeling that the parent is interfering or being pushy. Your children may well learn from your mistakes more effectively since you are always hovering over them and giving them advice every step of the way. Your children will most likely arrive on time, have their homework done promptly, and be prepared for their activities. They will be safe because you will always know where they are and with whom.

Many people are quick to criticize helicopter and snowplow parents as too controlling and overly domineering. They argue that this approach ends up having a detrimental effect on a child's development. However, I genuinely believe that these parents mean well and want the best for their children. In their defense, the world has become much more competitive — and that includes college admission requirements, sports teams, and so many more activities that require "making the team" to participate. They believe that their child's only way to excel is by pushing them hard and packing as many different activities into their days as possible, rather than just letting them be children and indulge in simple free play.

There is merit to this argument. Several years ago, I went to Philadelphia to take a test to become certified to teach tennis. I am a lifelong student of the game and a former recreational player. I even hired a personal trainer at one time to help get my game to the next level. It paid some dividends, and I eventually played a bit at level 4.5 after having won a couple of tournaments at level 4. If you follow the game, you know what these numbers mean. When I ventured into the coaching realm, I saw the game from a wholly different perspective. I would primarily coach younger children, but also some older adults and high school kids on occasion.

As much as the kids, one thing that stood out to me was the parents' varying levels of involvement. Some parents were, to put it mildly, very hands-on. They would watch my every move intently as I worked with their children. It was as if they were on the court with me, looking over my shoulder. It felt as though I could even smell their colognes and perfumes at times!

Other parents took the opposite approach. They dropped their kids off and then disappeared for an hour and a half. For all they knew, I could have spent the last hour and a half playing chess with their kids, and they would not have known.

From the court to the classroom, I have seen many students and coaches come and go, and I have some insight into what makes a champion. One common denominator, or so it seemed, among all the advanced players, was that they had very hands-on parents and very high-octane coaches. In many cases, these parents were obsessive about tennis, as were the coaches. They pushed their kids nonstop and employed plenty of tough love every step of the way. The result of this tough love was that often these kids were able to excel in the sport. Perhaps that amounted to Division 1 opportunities and potential scholarships. Would they have been able to have as much success as they did without the benefit of hard-driving, high octane, type-A parents and coaches? I am not so sure. Maybe effective parental advocacy is about figuring out what buttons to push.

There are, of course, some cons to helicopter and snowplow parenting. Your children may well grow up to be less independent and overly sheltered as adults. They may have trouble making their own decisions independently and continuously seek out approval from their parents. Their self-confidence may be affected to the point that they fear facing situations alone. Because they are not afforded the opportunity to learn from their mistakes growing up, they may well lack vital problem-solving skills needed for everyday life. They may also grow up with a sense of entitlement and take for granted that they will always be around people who love and care for them. They may well end up living their parent's dreams and ambitions, not their own. Sometimes, down the road, they may grow to resent their parents – or feel angst towards them – for controlling them. Thus, they may begin to rebel against their parents, more so when they see their peers growing up with so-called everyday parenting. Ultimately, they may feel limited or restricted by what their parents think are their maximum or minimum capabilities and not being allowed to try things for themselves.

Concerning the uninvolved or neglectful parent, there are also pros and cons. On the positive side, these children tend to learn self-reliance and take care of their essential needs early. Thus, they're equipped to handle situations where they have to be independent for prolonged periods. However, the drawbacks to this style far outweigh the good.

The children of an uninvolved parent may never develop an emotional connection with their parents. Lack of affection and attention at a young age can lead to low self-esteem or emotional neediness in other relationships. It can lead to a whole host of problems when your child sets foot on a college campus. This style of parenting may also affect a child's social skills. These children may have difficulties with social interaction outside the home because they never learn necessary communication and social skills from their parents. Moreover, they may lack the necessary coping skills. Ultimately, children who grow up with an emotional detachment from their parents may repeat this parenting style with their kids, and consequently, they may have the same poor relationship with their children. It is a vicious cycle. But you do not have to fall victim to it. Regardless of the reasons, it is possible to change a parenting style if you can notice it within yourself.

It might help to seek counseling to deal with mental health issues, past abuse, or other issues that prevent you from establishing an emotional bond with your child. It will not happen overnight. Unfortunately, it is not a quick-fix solution. Be patient. We are all works in progress.

I realize that some of you reading this may still have an aversion to counseling, and that is ok. As someone with a master's degree in counseling, I am the first to tell you that I do not think it is appropriate for everyone. The vital thing to consider is that you talk to someone more objective and impartial. Maybe that person is a minister at your church, a friend of a friend, an advocate, or whoever. Your goal is to solicit honest and unbiased feedback about who you are, and equally important, who you are not.

From Tough Love to Enough Love – How to Successfully Parent Your College Student

When their children prepare to leave for college, parents' emotions generally express themselves in one of two ways: "OMG, my baby is leaving the nest, and I am freaking out!" or, at the other end of the spectrum: "My baby is leaving the nest; finally, I get some alone time. Wahoo!"

Once your students set foot on a college campus, it can become one of the most challenging times for a parent. Your student will be entering a transformational phase of life, and you will no longer be able to see him or her as often to witness their transformation. You will probably have concerns about how your student is handling being away from home for the first time, how they are settling in, and whether they are adjusting to college life. If they are a commuter student and still living at home, you may have similar concerns about adapting to their new schedule. These are all legitimate concerns and to be expected. However, for your student to grow into his or her full potential as an individual, it is best if he or she must deal with new and different situations – many of which will present a problem-solving challenge – without running to you (at least as a first option). The following are some tips to for how to successfully parent your new college student:

I think first and foremost, the most important thing you can do for you – and your student – is to recognize and acknowledge that this is a time of ambivalence and change for parents and students alike. Change is often hard to embrace, as is stepping out of our comfort zones. In order to grow in life, we must be willing to take that step and allow our children to do the same. If you feel mixed emotions, maybe a sense of nostalgia combined with a sense of loss, reach out to other parents who are experiencing the same thing. There are plenty of parents experiencing the same emotions you are, and they are only a few clicks away.

Recognize that your student may be experiencing some of the very same conflicting emotions that you are. Maybe they feel as if they are stuck in between the past, present, and future, and that is ok. It is merely a sign of the ambivalent and transitional nature of this time of their life.

What Not to Do

Before I go into greater detail about successfully parenting your college-age student, I think it is equally important to shed some light on things you should avoid doing. As previously stated, sometimes we need to figure out who not to be before figuring out who we want to be.

Does this conversation sound familiar? "These are the best years of your life. You have no 'real' responsibilities. You have plenty of freedom.

You can even sleep in if you want to; this is as good as it gets, and blah, blah, blah ... " Of course you have. Many parents have told their college-age children these very same words. The fact is, no one – and I mean no one – is happy all the time between the ages of 18 and 22. When a student is homesick, fatigued from studying all night, or stressed out about roommate problems, finances, grades, etc., it is not very reassuring to have parents imply that this is as good as it gets! Sometimes we all want to be heard. We do not want to listen to people who are rendering value judgments all the time and offering so-called solutions, often in the form of empty platitudes. So, if your student has anxiety, do not deny them the opportunity to feel it. Let them experience it and own it. If you have ever studied mindfulness, you may be familiar with the phrase "just sit with it." Mindfulness suggests that the more we try to fight – or repress – feelings of anxiety, the more we exacerbate the problem. So, if you – or your student – feel pressure associated with this new transition, just accept it and "sit with it." It will begin to subside, slowly but surely. It will not happen overnight, it takes time to manage these emotions, but you will get there eventually. I know this sounds counterintuitive to most people; when we have a problem, our first instinct is to get rid of it, not merely sit with it. Why would we want to prolong this feeling any more than we must, right? But sometimes, the solution to the problem is not to offer a solution and to just accept it.

Avoid Too Much Advice

As Winston Churchill once so eloquently stated: "I love to learn, but I don't always like to be taught." Your student will inevitably get frustrated at some point during his or her time in college and likely complain to you about many different things: acerbic roommates, studying, money woes, and much more. Naturally, you will want to offer solutions, and you may well have all the answers. But I encourage you to refrain from advising unless they explicitly ask you what they should do. Even then, I would encourage you – to the extent possible – to help them help themselves and put the problem back in their hands. It is, after all, one of many golden opportunities for them to grow. Most likely, they just want someone who will listen without rendering judgment. They want to be heard and have a safe space to vent (don't we all?) and not someone to tell them what to do. To minimize conflicts and avoid having any blood spilled, just lend an ear, and let them know you are there to help if they ever need any advice on dealing with any issues, and leave it at that. By extending this overture, you are sending a message that you are standing by, ready to dispense advice, but only if they ask for it, and not only will you not come across as the bossy parent, but you will have created a safe space for your student.

When there comes a time to give advice, be sure to talk to them and not at them. If you speak at them or are condescending, they will block out your suggestion in a New York minute. It is essential to reflect on how your parents gave you advice when you were in the same life stage. What helped you, and what rubbed you the wrong way? Be mindful of this when talking to your kids. Ultimately, if they are not in any danger, there is no reason to meddle in their affairs, unless of course, they ask you for input.

Do Not Visit Too Often

If your student happens to be attending a college that is not too far away – or if their apartment or dorm room has a beautiful waterfront view overlooking the ocean with lots of palm trees in plain sight – you may be tempted to visit frequently. As I write this in the middle of January in Western New York, that sounds pretty tempting now. Try to limit your visits to not more than once per month at the most, and when you do, ask what they would like to do. Respect their time and space. Ensure that you make plans instead of just dropping by unannounced. It will send a signal that you appreciate their new lifestyle just as you would for any other adult who may well have plans.

Do Not Pressure Them to Come Home All the Time

Once you send your student off to college, it will be tempting to want to have them home all the time. You might feel a void in your life if you are now an empty nester, but you want your student to get the full college life experience. Although you will undoubtedly miss them, pressuring them to come home all the time does not serve their best interests. If they want to go home on the weekends, encourage them to stay on campus instead. Students who remain on campus only for classes and regularly return home tend to enjoy the college experience less because they are not as tied to the campus and the campus community. They never really get the opportunity to develop a connection and an identity with the campus community. There is plenty of research within academia that suggests that students who are the most successful in college are those students who feel connected with the campus or feel connected with the community. So, encourage your student to join some campus clubs or activities to get to know other students, which may help to connect them to their campus better, especially if they feel lonely or isolated.

The Parental Advocacy Tool Kit

Now that you have dropped your son or daughter off at college and you head home, it is time to start thinking about things you can do to enrich their college experience. First things first, recognize that the college years are a time for exploration and discovery. As such, do not be surprised if they show up at your doorstep with a new look: maybe they are wearing someone else's clothes, are ascribing to contemporary politics, philosophies, or even new eating habits. Do not despair. Take a step back, have a sense of humor, and just let them be themselves.

Keep in Touch – But Not Too Much

I believe there is an art to communication at any level. Authentic communication can only take place when we dare to be vulnerable. That means when we are willing to share the uncomfortable parts of our life, as much as the virtuous things. So, practice – and that is the operative word here – authentic exchanges with your children long before they ever set foot on a college campus.

When they finally get there, you will have created a foundation for authentic conversation, whether via phone or video chat (this would be the preferred method) or text or email. Recognize that it's vital for your student to become immersed in college life without you calling every hour to check on them. Remember, if you have established a solid foundation for communication built on real, authentic exchanges, you will not need to talk every hour to confirm this. As your student adjusts to college life, they will likely need someone to bounce ideas off of and be open to talking to them, but do not force things. Let them know that you can speak without judgment, no matter what the issue may be.

Communicate How You Are
Going to Communicate

You read that right. This idea may sound a bit over the top to some people — kind of like cleaning up before the cleaners come — but I think it is essential to be clear on expectations right from the very beginning. How you view communication happening and how they see things may be completely different? Do you want a planned time to talk, or do you want to be more spontaneous? Mobile phones are great, but some students see them as "electronic leashes." Email and text are often convenient, especially when you have younger children at home and cannot talk as often, but they are often easily misinterpreted and superficial. They present merely an illusion of connectedness. Indeed, concerning email and text, we are never as connected as we think we are.

Be an Anchor

Accepting changes must be a two-way street. College students want their parents to embrace all the changes in their lives, but they often wish for everything at home to stay the same. So, you must keep them abreast of all changes at home, whether that is moving a younger sibling into a new room, or maybe it is an illness in the family, a promotion at work, or even the death of a pet. They need this from you to feel secure, connected, and to maintain a sense of trust.

Make A Financial Plan and
Outline Your Expectations

To avoid any sticker shock, develop a tentative budget in advance and be clear about who will pay for what. For example, some parents agree to pay for books and supplies while their child is responsible for incidentals, such as snacks, movies, Netflix, etc. Other students are accountable for earning a percentage of their tuition. Teach your child about the responsible use of credit and debit cards, and encourage them to establish credit. It will make things easier for them down the road.

Acknowledge that College
Today is a Different Animal

The centuries-old buildings look the same, but college life today is quite different, even compared to 25 or 30 years ago. Things move much more quickly in the digital age, and with increased speed comes increased challenges. Students want what they want, and they wanted it yesterday. Work comes to them at a much faster rate. More is expected of them. Many students have been limited to online courses only this past year due to restrictions caused by the COVID-19 pandemic, and this can cause plenty of stress and anxiety for students. As I write this, college counseling centers are splitting at the seams, overflowing with appointments. Unfortunately, anxiety and depression are at all-time highs, which is certainly not limited to college campuses. Be mindful of this, and sensitive to the challenges your student may be facing. Invite them to share with you the discovery of new ideas, academic interests, and intellectual passions that may be brewing in their young minds.

Selected Bibliography

An, V. (2018, April 18). How to Negotiate a Financial Aid Package. Retrieved from https://www.northwesternmutual.com/life-and-money/how-to-negotiate-a-financial-aid-package/.

Apple, L. (2019, April 29). The Value of Financial Literacy and Self-Advocacy. Retrieved from https://blog.ed.gov/2019/04/the-value-of-financial-literacy-and-self-advocacy/.

Bromwich, J. & Miller C. (2019, March 16). How Parents Are Robbing Their Children of Adulthood. Retrieved from https://www.nytimes.com/2019/03/16/style/snowplow-parenting-scandal.html

Butler, J. (2020, December 11). 10 Tenancy Rights Every Student Should Know About. Retrieved from https://www.savethestudent.org/accommodation/what-are-your-rights-as-a-tenant.html.

Coburn, K. (2009, September 9). Letting Go: Tips for Parents of New College Students. Retrieved from https://www.greatschools.org/gk/articles/letting-go-new-college-students/.

Cunningham, K. (2020, January 21). What Are Your Rights as A Student? Retrieved from https://www.rewire.org/rights-college-student/.

D'Alessio, K. & Osterholt, D. (2018, August 7). Cultivating Self-Advocacy for All Students on

College Campuses. Retrieved from
https://nebhe.org/journal/cultivating-self-advocacy-for-all-students-on-college-campuses/.

Elias, M. (2019, October 2). Know Your Rights: A Crash Course on Title IX. Retrieved from https://www.avoicefortheinnocent.org/know-your-rights-a-crash-course-on-title-ix/.

English, B. (2013, November 9). Snowplow Parents Overly Involved in College Students Lives. Retrieved from
https://www.bostonglobe.com/arts/2013/11/09/parents-overly-involved-college-students-lives/mfYvA5R9IhRpJytEbFpxUP/story.html.

Erblat, A. (2013, September 24). A Guide to Your Rights When Dealing with Campus Police Officers. Retrieved from
https://www.upressonline.com/2013/09/a-guide-to-your-rights-when-dealing-with-campus-police-officers/.

Fuld, J. (2018, November 26) Community Advocacy Basics: A Beginner's Guide to Advocacy. Retrieved from
https://www.thecampaignworkshop.com/blog/pillar/advocacy-campaigns/community-advocacy.

Gibson, C. (2017, March 30). What Are the Benefits of Being Part of an Advocacy Collaborative? Retrieved from
https://grantcraft.org/content/blog/what-are-the-benefits-of-being-part-of-an-advocacycollaborative/#:~:text=Fellow%20grantmakers%20from%20institutions%20with,than%20they%20can%20do%20individually.

Gray, P. (2015, October 23). Helicopter Parenting & College Students' Increased Neediness. Retrieved from https://www.psychologytoday.com/us/blog/freedom-learn/201510/helicopter-parenting-college-students-increased-neediness.

Grutta, C. (2018, May 6). Advising Perspective: Teaching Students to Self-Advocate. Retrieved from https://www.landmark.edu/research-training/blog/advising-perspective-teaching-students-to-self-advocate

Habash, T. & Shireman, R. (2016, April 28). How Enrollment Contracts Limit Students' Rights. Retrieved from https://tcf.org/content/report/how-college-enrollment-contracts-limit-students-rights/?agreed=1.

Higuera, V. (2019, September 12). What is Helicopter Parenting? Retrieved from https://www.healthline.com/health/parenting/helicopter-parenting

Higuera, V. (2019, September 20). What is Uninvolved Parenting? Retrieved from https://www.healthline.com/health/parenting/uninvolved-parenting.

Hoyt, E. (2018, June 13). How to Successfully Parent Your College Student. Retrieved from https://www.fastweb.com/college-search/articles/how-to-successfully-parent-your-college-student.

Khoury, G. (2017, June 15). Dealing with Campus Police: Top 3 Legal FAQs for College

Students. Retrieved from https://blogs.findlaw.com/blotter/2017/06/dealing-with-campus-police-top-3-legal-faq-for-college-students.html.

Kouros, Chrisyna D. (2017, September 15). 6 Tips for Parenting College Students. Retrieved from https://www.nextavenue.org/parenting-college-students/

Krakauer, J. (2015) Missoula: Rape and the Justice System in a College Town. New York: Doubleday, a division of Penguin Random House LLC

Narayanan, L. (2020, January 13). 4 Advocacy Examples to Get You Inspired. Retrieved from https://callhub.io/advocacy-campaigns-examples/

Porter, E. (2018, August 30). Talking to Teachers: Building Self-Advocacy in College Students. Retrieved from https://www.beyondbooksmart.com/executive-functioning-strategies-blog/talking-to-teachers-building-self-advocacy-in-college-students

Rich, B. (2019, February 12). Bullying In College- Awareness, Outreach and Prevention. Retrieved from https://thebestschools.org/magazine/bullying-in-college/

Watkins, R. (2020, November 26). Knowing Your Rights With Campus Police. Retrieved from https://thecollegepost.com/campus-police-rights/

Witz, Billy (2020, November 21). "A Walk-On Opted Out. Then Came a $24,000.00 Bill." The New York Times.

35 Measurable Self Advocacy/Self Determination IEP Goals. (n.d.) Retrieved from https://adayinourshoes.com/self-advocacy-iep-goals/

Procedures for Handling Student Complaints about Faculty Conduct In Academic Settings. (2010). Retrieved from https://www.cuny.edu/wp-content/uploads/sites/4/page-assets/about/administration/offices/legal-affairs/policies-procedures/Student-Complaints-About-Faculty-Conduct-in-Academic-Settings.pdf

The Pros and Cons of Helicopter Parenting (2016, June 22). Retrieved from https://parentsworld.com.sg/2016/06/22/the-pros-and-cons-of-helicopter-parenting/

Student Codes of Conduct: Background (2016). Retrieved from https://www.findlaw.com/education/student-conduct-and-discipline/student-codes-of-conduct-background.html

Scholarship and Financial Aid Scams (2012). Retrieved from https://www.consumer.ftc.gov/articles/0082-scholarship-and-financial-aid-scams

The Top Mental Health Challenges Facing Students (2020). Retrieved from https://www.bestcolleges.com/resources/top-5-mental-health-problems-facing-college-students/

The Advantages of Advocacy (n.d.). Retrieved from https://www.open.edu/openlearncreate/mod/oucontent/view.php?id=175&section=20.5

The Top 3 Benefits of Advocacy (2015, January 15). Retrieved from https://imaleadership.wordpress.com/2015/01/20/top-3-benefits-of-advocacy/

Ways to Practice Self-Advocacy in the Virtual Classroom. (2020 April 15). Retrieved fromhttps://www.perkinselearning.org/technology/blog/ways-practice-self-advocacy-virtual-classroom

Advocating for Financial Aid Programs: How to Get Involved. (2017, April 11). Retrieved from https://medium.com/nyu-affordability/advocating-for-student-financial-aid-programs-how-to-get-involved-89d37401a18a

Values Clarification (2021). Retrieved from https://www.therapistaid.com/therapy-worksheet/values-clarification`

Vanderbilt University (n.d.). Clery Act Frequently Asked Questions. Retrieved from https://police.vanderbilt.edu/crimeinfo/cleryactfaq.php

What is the Implied Warranty of Habitability? (2016, June 20). Retrieved from https://www.findlaw.com/realestate/landlord-tenant-law/what-is-the-implied-warranty-of-habitability.html

Student Housing Laws College Students Should Now (2017, December 19). Retrieved from https://www.findlaw.com/education/higher-education/student-housing-laws-college-students-should-know.html

What is the Clery Act? (2012, September 24). Retrieved from

https://www.bostonglobe.com/metro/2012/09/24/what-clery-act/BUUayEMxlLa8MByNRmmtRP/story.html#:~:text=It%20is%20intended%20to%20protect,to%20a%20designated%20campus%20official.

Dean of Students. 10 Academic Rights (n.d.). Retrieved from https://studentaffairs.unt.edu/dean-of-students

Academic Grievance Policy and Procedures for Undergraduate Students. University of Buffalo. (2020, November 17). Retrieved from https://catalog.buffalo.edu/policies/academic_grievance_policy_and_procedures_for_undergraduate_students.html

About the Author

Dr. Rich Schlesinger teaches Career Explorations, Communications, and First-Year Experience Courses at Genesee Community College in Batavia, NY. He has over 25 years of higher education experience as an administrator, teacher, counselor, and career management consultant in the public and private sector. He resides in Buffalo, NY. For further information, contact Dr. Schlesinger at rschlesinger66@gmail.com

Acknowledgements

Thank you to Andrea Seydel for her invaluable input, advice, insight, and support, for putting up with me, and for agreeing to join me on this journey. Thank you to Lindy Bailey for polishing what needed to be polished. Thank you to Teddy Fakles for her wisdom and creativity. Thank you to Cathy Petruccione and Lori Bakos Kubik for tooting my horn. Thank you to Ryan and Lauren for inspiring me each and every day. I love you both very much!

About the Publisher:

Publish Your Book with Ease, Speed and Professionalism!

I bet the world of publishing seems confusing. After searching for options, you are overwhelmed, unsure and confused about the direction to take, but know you want to bring your book to the world.

You questioned the likelihood of getting published by a large publishing house and are worried about the stigma or lack of credibility with self-publishing.

You appreciate the big publishers' professionalism but know the chances of getting published by them are slim to none.

You enjoy the total royalties of self-publishing but don't want to figure out the whole process yourself.

What if there was an efficient, professional way to publish your book without having to figure out the entire process and where you could keep all your royalties and be a part of a reputable publishing company?

What if there was an easy way you could get fast to market in all distribution channels and bookstores while still being able to see your sales and royalties?

Let Live Life Happy (LLH) Be Your Publishing Company That Helps You Turn Your Dream Into Achievement Through Book-Birthing!

Founder of Live Life Happy Publishing, Andrea Seydel, helps expectant authors painlessly give birth to their books. Her clients lovingly call her The Book Doula. She is an eight-time Best-Selling author, writing coach and founder of LLH Publishing.

Live Life Happy Publishing house bridges the gap between traditional and self-publishing with high standards, quality production, and industry knowledge.

This hybrid approach offers the same quality, credibility and customer reach that traditional publishing offers while maintaining the freedom, total royalties and fast-to-market service that self-publishing brings. If you are looking for a modern professional approach to publishing, consider The Book Doula and her hybrid publishing option to walk you through the steps of book publishing.

At the end of the process, you will have a professionally published book in your hand that anyone can purchase from around the world.

Books change lives, whose life will you touch with your book?

Please set up a discovery call today! Let's get you one step closer to your dream of becoming a published author.

www.andreaseydel.com

Made in the USA
Middletown, DE
17 June 2022